HUGH ALLEY'S CAVEAT

The London Topographical Society
and the editors of this volume
would like to thank the Committee of
the Isobel Thornley Bequest Fund for
a generous grant towards the cost
of publication.

HUGH ALLEY'S CAVEAT

The Markets of London in 1598

Folger Ms V. a. 318

Edited by

IAN ARCHER

CAROLINE BARRON

VANESSA HARDING

London Topographical Society

Publication No. 137

1988

© London Topographical Society

Publication No. 137 of the
London Topographical Society
3 Meadway Gate, London NW11

ISBN 0 902087 23 1

General Editor: Ann Loreille Saunders PhD, FSA

PRINTED IN GREAT BRITAIN BY
W. S. MANEY AND SON LTD, HUDSON ROAD, LEEDS

CONTENTS

TO THE COURTEOUS READER

We have compiled this book together, and shared information, but each of us is primarily responsible for one or more sections of the introduction and notes. Caroline Barron sought out the manuscript in the Folger Library, and first thought of publishing it, with notes; Ann Saunders of the London Topographical Society encouraged the idea, and Ian Archer and Vanessa Harding joined to write about areas of particular interest to them. Vanessa Harding wrote about the history of the markets and market regulation, and the history of the manuscript; Ian Archer wrote the section on Hugh Alley and his proposals for reform of the market; Caroline Barron compiled the detailed commentary on the plates, and wrote about the value of the manuscript.

We would like to thank The Folger Shakespeare Library for permission to reproduce Hugh Alley's 'Caveat', and Laetitia Yeandle there for her help. We are grateful for the assistance we have received, as always, from the staff of the Corporation of London Records Office, and also from the staff of Guildhall Library (Maps and Prints), Westminster Public Library (Archives Department), and the British Museum (Prints and Drawings). The map of the London markets is based, with permission, on an outline drawn by the Department of Urban Archaeology of the Museum of London. We have benefited from criticism and advice from John Walter and Penry Williams, and Martha Carlin, David Crouch, Derek Keene, James Robertson, and John Schofield have made valuable comments and suggestions and allowed us to draw on their unpublished work. Professor Mark Benbow's index of London citizens involved in City government, 1558–1603 (in preparation), has been of especial value to us. Finally, we are grateful to Ann Saunders, Editor of the London Topographical Society, for her time, patience, enthusiasm, and splendid cooking.

January 1988

IAN ARCHER
CAROLINE BARRON
VANESSA HARDING

ABBREVIATIONS

APC	*Acts of Privy Council of England*, ed. J. R. Dasent (32 vols, 1890–1907)
A–Z	*The A to Z of Elizabethan London*, compiled by A. Prockter and R. Taylor (LTS 1979)
Beaven	A. B. Beaven, *The Aldermen of the City of London, temp. Henry III–1912* (2 vols, 1908, 1913)
Benbow, Index	R. M. Benbow, Index of London Citizens involved in City Government, 1558–1603 (in preparation)
BL	British Library
CEMCR	*Calendar of Early Mayor's Court Rolls of the City of London, 1298–1307*, ed. A. H. Thomas (1924)
CCPR	CLRO, Search Room, Card Calendar of Property References
CLBA etc.	*Calendar of Letter Books A to L*, ed. R. R. Sharpe (11 vols, 1899–1912)
CLRO	Corporation of London Records Office
CPMR	*Calendar of Plea and Memoranda Rolls of the City of London, 1322–1482* (6 vols), ed. A. H. Thomas (1926–43) and P. E. Jones (1954–61)
Dietz	*The Port and Trade of Early Elizabethan London: documents*, ed. B. Dietz (LRS 8, 1972)
DNB	*Dictionary of National Biography*
GL	Guildhall Library
Harben	H. A. Harben, *A Dictionary of London* (1918)
H of C.	*The House of Commons 1558–1603*, vols i–iii, ed. P. W. Hasler (1986)
HTA, Gazetteer	*Historic Towns Atlas: Medieval London* ed. M. D. Lobel (forthcoming, 1988)
Journal	CLRO, Journals of the Court of Common Council and the Court of Aldermen, from 1416
Letterbook	CLRO, Letterbooks, from 1275
Lib. Alb.	*Liber Albus (Munimenta Gildhallae Londoniensis)*, ed. H. T. Riley (Rolls series 12, parts 1 and 3, 1859–62)
Lib. Cust.	*Liber Custumarum (Munimenta Gildhallae Londoniensis)*, ed. H. T. Riley (Rolls series 12, part 2, 1860)
LRS	London Record Society
LTR	*London Topographical Record*
LTS	London Topographical Society
Memorials	*Memorials of London and London life in the 13th, 14th, and 15th centuries*, ed. H. T. Riley (1868)
OED	*Oxford English Dictionary* (1933)
PRO	Public Record Office
Rep.	CLRO, Repertories of the Court of Aldermen, from 1495
Stow	John Stow, *A Survey of London* (2nd edn, 1603; ed. C. L. Kingsford, 1908, repr. 1971)
TLAMAS	*Transactions of the London and Middlesex Archaeological Society*
WPL	Westminster Public Library

INTRODUCTION

The manuscript here reproduced is a small paper volume of twenty-three folios, 17 × 23 cm, entitled 'A Caveatt for the Citty of London, OR a forewarning of offences against penall Lawes' and dated 1598. It comprises a dedication to the then Lord Mayor, a foreword 'to the curteous reader', and a series of pen and wash pictures of the city's markets, with on the facing pages depictions (possibly portraits) in colour of the alderman and deputy of the ward in which each market was situated. There are also pen and wash pictures of four of the city gates. The author gives his name as Hugh Alley, citizen and Plaisterer of London; in the foreword he speaks rather ambiguously of 'the poore painter' and 'the paynter with his pensile', perhaps implying that the artwork is not all his own, but if this is the case his collaborator remains anonymous.[1]

In the dedication and foreword Alley outlines his concern at abuses in the city's marketing system, and proposes, without ever clearly defining, reforms and preventive measures. The drawings show thirteen of London's food markets, and add in what must be part of his scheme for reform: pillars to define the standings of the country traders, and columns or monuments where market offenders were to be punished, or at least their offences publicised. The activities at the city's gates are also perhaps part of the plan to control marketing more effectively.

Hugh Alley's real motivation for writing and presenting the *Caveat*, the exact purpose he hoped to achieve thereby, and the effect it actually did have, are not apparent in the document itself, but are illuminated by study of the historical context. In this introduction we discuss briefly the history of the city's markets, and the way in which food was sold in London, and in greater detail Alley's career, the system of informing and prosecuting market offences in the later sixteenth century, and the food shortages of the 1590s, which form the immediate background to this work. General comments on the drawings, their historical and topographical value, and on the history of the manuscript, are followed by a transcript of the text of the *Caveat*, and by reproductions of the whole manuscript, with a detailed commentary on each plate.

NOTES

[1] This point is discussed below, p. 32.

THE LONDON FOOD MARKETS

The London food markets shown in Hugh Alley's *Caveat* of 1598 were still largely on the sites established by 1300; it was only in the seventeenth century that the City tried to rearrange and relocate its markets to serve the expanding population better.[1] Some system of markets and market regulation probably existed before the Norman conquest, but details of where they were and how they operated are generally lacking till the period of better written records.

THE MEDIEVAL MARKETS

Queenhithe and Billingsgate were ports, landing places for goods, including foodstuffs, brought by water, by the early eleventh century.[2] We do not know whether at this early date they were also the scene of market activity, buying and selling, or whether the goods landed were transported to other places in the city for retail. The street names of Westcheap (modern Cheapside) and Eastcheap are clearly Anglo-Saxon in linguistic origin,[3] but again we do not know whether the buying and selling that the names imply included the marketing of food, though it seems very probable. The names of streets nearby, though not of such obviously early origins, are suggestive: Milk Street, Bread Street, and Honey Lane off Cheapside, Pudding Lane (taking its name from butchers' offal) off Eastcheap.[4]

While in principle the whole town was a place of sale, it was common for certain areas to become the 'accustomed places' where goods of various types, especially food, were sold. The two main food market areas of the city lay west and east of the Walbrook. The western market probably occupied the whole length of the thoroughfare from Newgate to the Walbrook, but focused on Cheapside or Westcheap; in the east there appears to have been food marketing in Eastcheap, in Bridge Street–Gracechurch Street, and along Cornhill. It is not clear at what date certain places in London became identified as the sites of specialist markets for grain, flesh, fish, and other foodstuffs, but there are references to the churches of St Nicholas at the shambles (*apud Macellum*: St Nicholas Shambles, near Newgate) and St Nicholas in the west fish market (*[in] Westpiscariam*:

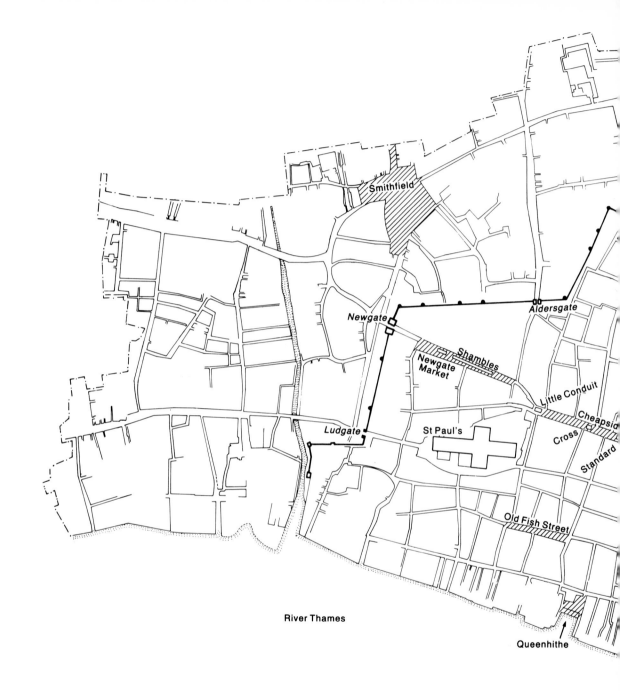

Smithfield

Newgate

Shambles

Newgate Market

Aldersgate

Little Conduit

Cheapside

Ludgate

St Paul's

Cross

Standard

Old Fish Street

River Thames

Queenhithe

0   2000 ft

0   500m

*Figure 1   Map of the pre-Fire City of London, showing
the approximate sites of the markets in 1598*

N

‎olegate

Moorgate

Bishopsgate

Bishopsgate Street

Great Conduit

Cornhill

Stocks

Leadenhall Street

Conduit

Leadenhall

Aldgate

Gracechurch Street

Conduit
East Cheap

New Fish Street

Tower

Billingsgate

Southwark

St Nicholas Cole Abbey) in the twelfth century. By the end of the twelfth century the western fish market seems to have moved from Cheapside to Old Fish Street, south of St Paul's, but it was still a street market.[5]

Most of the specialised medieval food markets, as we understand them, were in existence by the middle of the thirteenth century: in the west, the shambles by Newgate, the Old Fish Market, and Cheapside as a general market; in the east, the butchery of Eastcheap, the fish market in Bridge Street (New Fish Street, now Fish Street Hill), and a general market probably in Cornhill and perhaps Gracechurch Street. There were four grain markets, two on the waterside at Queenhithe and Billingsgate and two inland, again one west (Newgate Street) and one east (by the fourteenth century in Gracechurch Street, probably originally in Cornhill).[6] Smithfield, outside the walls, had a market for livestock and horses on Fridays by the time of FitzStephen (*c.*1180), and remained a livestock market for the medieval and early modern periods.[7]

The waterfront of the city was obviously an important centre for trade, with the grain markets of Queenhithe and Billingsgate, and the fishwharves associated with the inland fish markets. Much of the city's provisions came by water, as well as the commodities of overseas trade, and some goods, including grain, shellfish, wine, hay and straw, were sold from the boats in which they came, as well as at the landing-places.[8]

These early markets were in the streets of the city, and as the city's population grew in the thirteenth century they probably began to cause something of a nuisance. It may have been this, among other factors, which prompted some re-organisation of the markets in the late thirteenth century in anticipation of Edward I's visit to the city in 1274. The mayor, Henry le Waleys, ordered the stalls of the butchers and fishmongers and others to be removed from Cheapside 'lest any filth should remain in Cheap against the coming of the king, who in a short time, as it is said, was to come from foreign parts to the city ... and he assigned them to sell their wares in other places'.[9]

The new place assigned to the butchers and fishmongers was on open ground at Woolchurchhaw, near the Walbrook crossing, where Threadneedle Street, Cornhill, and Lombard Street meet with Poultry. On this site, given by the Crown, le Waleys built a covered market, called 'Hales, *Anglice*

Stockes'[10] or *les Stokkes*,[11] which was specifically for meat and fish, with a number of stalls inside and out which were to be let out to butchers and fishmongers on a long-term basis. The rents of the market went to the upkeep of London Bridge. The new market seems to have been complete by 1283, when it was leased to a group of fishmongers, who were to sublet the stalls to butchers and fishmongers; the lease specifically stated that no other stalls for these commodities would be permitted elsewhere in the city, except in the accustomed places of Bridge Street (Fish Street Hill), Eastcheap, Old Fish Street, and 'the street of the butchers to the west in the parish of St. Nicholas' (the shambles by Newgate).[12]

At the same time le Waleys appears to have reorganised the meat market near Newgate. The king granted the city an empty plot near St Paul's churchyard, between 'the great gate of the churchyard opposite the church of St. Nicholas', and another gate in the wall of the churchyard opposite Ivy Lane, to build on and put to rent for the upkeep of London Bridge.[13] This may have been the origin of the 'middle row' of the Shambles meat market.

Civic interest in the markets in the fourteenth century was mostly confined to regulation of their locations and hours, and the price and quality of goods sold there; it is clear that despite the provision of new market buildings there was a tendency for trading to spill over into adjacent streets.[14] Further building works took place in the fifteenth century, at the Stocks and the new granary of Leadenhall. The Stocks market house was rebuilt in 1406–11, and it is this substantial stone building which is shown in Alley's drawing. There were stalls on the ground floor, probably as before, with rooms above, let out to merchants and others for the storage of their wares.[15]

Leadenhall was a great private house until its acquisition by the city in the fifteenth century, but food was being sold at or near there in the early fourteenth century: in 1310 the 'common market' upon Cornhill (as the part of Leadenhall Street extending from the Bishopsgate Street crossroads to St Mary Axe or Lime Street was then called) was mentioned.[16] In 1341 country poulterers were selling their wares there.[17] Leadenhall itself was bought by the city in 1411, and rebuilt as a granary and market in the 1440s, perhaps in response to a short-term grain shortage. It was an enclosed courtyard building, several storeys high, with an open space inside in which most of the market traders seem to have stood. The 'common market' for poultry, victuals, grain, eggs, butter, and cheese which used to be held 'at Leadenhall' was moved inside by order of Common Council in March 1455.[18]

Both of these houses were used for other purposes: the upper rooms at the Stocks were let to drapers, and cloth was sold there in 1380.[19] In the fifteenth century Leadenhall also became a centre where wool was weighed before sale, and lead, nails, and worsteds were stored and sold there from 1463. Later it became an important market for cloth and leather, on the days when the food markets were not open. The building was used for a variety of purposes apart from the food markets in the sixteenth century.[20]

It was not clear at first whether the city's markets belonged (together with the right to their tolls and profits) to the king, because they occupied the king's highway, or to the City, by concession with other royal rights. In 1244 the City claimed that the stalls in the highway had been granted to the citizens along with the right to elect their own sheriffs, in return for the annual farm or rent, but this may not have been accurate.[21] In 1266 and 1268, when the city was being directly ruled by the king, the bailiffs (in place of the sheriffs) accounted to the king's Exchequer for stallage and customs of the butchers and others selling in Westcheap and elswhere, and for issues from Gracechurch, Billingsgate, and the field of 'Smedfeld'.[22] The City did however have a clear title to some of the markets: Queenhithe was held by specific grant for an annual rent or farm, and the new markets of the Stocks and Leadenhall were also the City's. The City claimed rents from citizen poulterers holding standings in Newgate Street in the fourteenth century.[23] Henry IV by his charter of 1400 granted to the city the collection of tolls and customs in Cheap, Billingsgate, and Smithfield, and perhaps it was only from this date that the city exercised undisputed jurisdiction over all the markets; certainly in the fifteenth and sixteenth centuries it seems to have run them all, and taken rents and profits, without hindrance. The charter of 1327 granted that no market was to be held within seven miles of the city, and with the exception of Southwark and the declining market at Westminster, this seems to have remained true until the seventeenth century.[24]

MARKET REGULATION AND OFFENCES

The markets in London included both defined areas where citizens could open shops and stalls to deal in a particular food commodity, and street markets where country traders could bring their produce for sale. The definition of citizenship became more precise in the thirteenth century, but there would always have been a recognisable distinction between residents and householders of London, and country people coming to trade temporarily. Only citizens could open permanent shops, and only they could deal extensively with citizens and non-citizens alike; non-citizens ('foreigns') could not trade with one another.[25] But even the citizens' freedom was restricted, because the London markets, as markets everywhere, were hedged about with regulations.

The aim of market regulations, in London as elsewhere, was primarily to ensure openness and fairness of dealing, and to protect the consumer from high prices and sharp practice. They sought to bring trading into the public eye, by limiting the time and place in which buying and selling could occur, and proscribed certain practices which undermined the freedom of the market. The interest of both the Crown and the City in the markets is reflected in regulations issued to control their operation: the city seems to have taken responsibility for overseeing and regulating the market on a day to day basis, but the king might intervene if it seemed that this responsibility was not being carried out.[26]

The main offences against the freedom of the markets were forestalling, engrossing, and regrating; each of these has a specific implication, but they could overlap. 'Forestalling' was going out before the market and buying from those who would otherwise have brought the goods to the market themselves. 'Engrossing' was buying up the whole, or a large part of, the stock of a particular commodity, with the implication of selling again at an enhanced price, while 'regrating' was buying goods in one market for resale in another. In principle these were offences which could be committed in respect of any kind of commodity for sale, but in practice we hear of them mostly in connection with victuals.[27]

The principle was that the producer should market his or her own produce, without the intervention of middlemen or dealers. Dealing in food was not entirely forbidden: some practices, such as buying in the market for resale in shops or by hucksters walking the street, were legal but restricted to certain persons or times. 'Regrating' sometimes meant simply this, not an actual infringement of market practice. 'Hawking', walking the streets to sell goods, was forbidden for some commodities, but was a legitimate activity for others: women known as 'regratresses' sold bread from the bakers, and in 1388 *birlesters* (also women) were allowed to sell oysters, mussels, salt fish and other victuals in the streets, but only if they kept moving.[28] This distinction between market trading and street selling was an important one, and long preserved: in 1588 the officer of the market and the constables and beadles of the wards were ordered to make sure that the fishwives who bought fish, oysters, mussels, cockles, and such like at Billingsgate did not stand in the market-places to sell them but walked up and down the streets crying them.[29]

Offences against the freedom of the market also included buying and selling outside the defined market hours. Methods of sale (by sample or otherwise) were regulated, and official weights, measures, and balances were prescribed.[30] The 'statutes of Smithfield', probably of late thirteenth-century date, specified the manner of doing a deal and payment on the spot for market goods including corn and meat, wherever they were sold.[31] The holder of the market, in London's case the mayor as representative of the commonalty, could prosecute for infringement of these regulations, and sentence offenders, especially the sellers of bad, unwholesome, or 'putrid' foods, to exemplary punishment in the pillory.[32]

The exact bounds of the medieval London markets, arising as most of them did in a period for which there is no written record, are usually a little unclear. It was probably only when they expanded beyond what were felt to be 'traditional' limits that the city tooks steps to define them, and to prevent their spreading further; but this may also reflect the greater attention paid to defining and recording city custom and the city's rights in general in the later medieval period. In 1364 the two areas of the waterfront at which fish might be landed were defined; in 1379 the bounds of Smithfield were given.[33] In 1414 the extent of the market areas in Eastcheap and Old Fish Street was defined, by reference to named properties and residents.[34]

It is clear that there were strict rules for the days and hours of market trading, but we often do not know what these were in the medieval period; probably no market was open six days a week, and most closed at noon. A proclamation in 1442–3 forbad the bringing of victuals into the city for sale on Sundays, whether by citizens or non-citizens, but it is clear that earlier it had been legal to sell meat on Sundays up to 10 a.m., and certainly later, in the sixteenth century, some selling of food was taking place on Sundays, whether legitimately or not.[35] The grain markets took place on Mondays, Wednesdays, and Fridays, opening at Prime in Newgate and Gracechurch Street and at half Prime in the waterside markets of Queenhithe and Billingsgate.[36] The poultry markets opened at Matins, but the first period of trading was for shoppers to buy for their own consumption; only after Prime could citizen poulterers, cooks, and regrators (in this context meaning hucksters) buy to resell. The foreign traders had to leave at noon.[37] Foreign fruiterers could only sell on three (later four) days a week, before noon.[38]

The butchers' markets were probably not open on Fridays, nor during Lent: accounts for the rents from the Stocks market show the latter clearly. In 1378 the butchers were instructed to shut their shops before dark ('before the time for candles being lighted') and forbidden to sell by candlelight.[39] According to FitzStephen, the horse market or fair at Smithfield took place on Fridays in the twelfth century, but by the sixteenth century the cattle and other livestock market was held there on Wednesdays as well.[40] There is better information on market days and times for the sixteenth century, but it seems clear that by then the customary market hours were changing.

Although the city authorities were anxious to preserve the markets from price-raising through restrictive practices, they did not allow them to operate with complete freedom, and intervened to set retail prices for a wide range of commodities. The price of bread was determined by the procedures of the city's assize of bread; fish and poultry of various kinds were listed and priced, and possibly meat was too.[41] It is not clear on what basis these prices were fixed: the assize of bread allowed for variations in the price of wheat, which presumably itself reflected supply and demand, but in setting retail prices for poultry and fish the mayor and Aldermen may have been trying to control wholesale prices as well.[42] If the set price was offered by a purchaser, the vendor had to accept it, and market traders were forbidden, once goods had been brought to a market, to take them away unsold and try to sell them elsewhere or on another day.[43]

Regulation of London's medieval markets required the participation of a large number of persons. Some of these were of semi-official status, such as the bailiffs of Queenhithe, Billingsgate, and Smithfield, and the sworn meters of grain, salt, and other commodities.[44] In several cases, though, the members of the City Company concerned were immediately in charge, in the same way that other companies oversaw the production and quality of goods other than food. Thus the Fish-mongers helped to set prices and punish sellers of bad fish; the wardens of the Butchers' Company were responsible for disposing of the filth and offal produced by the slaughter of beasts at Eastcheap and the Shambles.[45]

The city was concerned to regulate the sale of food and drink everywhere in the city, not only in the markets. The assize of bread, dating from the thirteenth century, covered the manufacture, types, weight, and price of bread; it was to be sold in the markets and not from the bakehouses, though these seem to have been located all over the city. The city bakers seem to have employed regratresses as well, to sell in the streets. Country bakers also sold bread in the markets, which they brought in carts; they too were subject to the assize.[46] The activities of the cooks, pastelers, and piebakers of Bread Street and Eastcheap, who sold food on the spot, as well as acting as contracted caterers for dinners and feasts, were closely regu-lated. Ale and wine were sold in alehouses and taverns, and qualities, prices, and the circumstances of sale were specified.[47] In the fifteenth century, and possibly earlier, it seems to have been the custom to appoint annually two of the Aldermen to supervise hostellers, brewers, cooks, pie-bakers, hucksters, and braziers or food retailers, to ensure that they observed the prices and hours laid down.[48]

THE MARKETS, FOURTEENTH TO SIXTEENTH CENTURIES

The rich documentation surviving from the fourteenth century and onwards gives us a good picture of activity in the various markets in the later medieval and early modern period. Regulations covered the marketing of particular commodities wherever they were sold, and the operation of the individual market places, which varied in hours, the variety of goods on sale, the traders entitled to sell there, and the accommodation offered. The London markets ranged from the temporary standings in Cheapside, occupied by the country traders with their carts and baskets, and the (removable) stalls in front of citizens' shops, to the shops themselves, and the permanent stalls including the middle row in Newgate Shambles and the fixed stalls within the Stocks market house. Leadenhall, a permanent building, indeed one of considerable size and splendour, accommodated markets in different commodities on different days, and was probably cleared every night, though permanent stalls appeared later.

THE MEAT MARKETS

The 'butchers' markets' of the medieval city sold beef, mutton, veal, and pork, but the general markets sold other meats, including poultry, rabbits, bacon and perhaps lamb. The city seems to have been keen to preserve the distinction, but not always successful in doing so. The history of meat marketing in London seems to be one of continual conflict between the citizen butchers and the country butchers, over access to the markets, and between the butchers and the city, on environ-mental grounds.[49]

Until the fifteenth or possibly the sixteenth century there were three butchers' markets, at Eastcheap, Newgate Shambles, and the Stocks; later Leadenhall became one too. Only the first two were places of slaughter, but the disposal of the butchers' waste there was a major environmental problem. Later there were attempts to ban slaughtering within the walls of the city, but not with any marked success.[50] The Stocks market developed as a butchers' market from the general market of Cheapside nearby, being set up to accommodate the butchers and fishmongers who had formerly stood in the street.[51]

Leadenhall was at first only a general market, and may not have become a flesh market until the late fifteenth or sixteenth century. Certainly its predecessor, the Cornhill market, was not recognised as a butchers' market.[52] In 1533 the country butchers selling from stalls in Leadenhall Street were ordered to sell from the stalls set up within the courtyard, but in 1540 they were again allowed to sell in the street. In 1546 all foreign butchers and others selling flesh (beef, mutton, veal, pork, and lamb) were ordered to sell at the stalls in Leadenhall, on Wednesdays and Saturdays; citizen butchers could sell at St Nicholas Shambles, the Stocks and Eastcheap. In 1548, however, the citizen butchers complained that the non-free butchers were still selling beef and mutton in the general markets, and petitioned that they should be forbidden to do so.[53]

Eastcheap and the Shambles were street markets: the former was lined with permanent shops, the latter included a 'middle row' of stalls which may have originated in the late thirteenth century. The bounds of Eastcheap market were given in 1414, and those of both markets in 1512: Eastcheap market stretched from Crooked Lane to Pudding Lane, the Newgate Shambles along the middle row and on both sides facing it.[54] The Stocks had permanent stalls, mostly inside but with some outside, the rents of which went to the City; in Leadenhall by the end of the sixteenth century there seem to have been permanent and privately owned stalls for butchers.[55]

THE FISH MARKETS

The history of fish marketing in London is complicated. The fishmongers seem to have been an unusually powerful guild or association in the early medieval period, and resisted attempts to open their trade to non-citizens. They occupied the shops in Old Fish Street and New Fish Street (now Fish Street Hill), as well as the stalls at the Stocks, and there seems to have been no provision for foreign (non-citizen) fishmongers to retail in these markets; their role was confined to bringing fish to the city for sale wholesale at the wharves to the city fishmongers. An enquiry in 1321 into the practices of the fishmongers concluded that there should be no retail sale of fish at the wharves, only in the 'three places especially set apart for the sale of fish by retail' in the markets of Bridge Street, Old Fish Street, and the Stocks. The fishmongers who had shops at the Fishwharf by St Magnus church, and who thereby gained an advantage over other fishmongers, contested this restriction on their freedom to sell. It was also noted that the poor of the city came to the Fishwharf to buy fish for resale by hawking in the streets.[56] In the case of corn, brought wholesale to the city in the same way as fish, citizens were allowed to buy for their own use from the

wholesale markets on the waterfront, but this does not seem to have applied to sea-fish.[57]

In the later fourteenth century attempts were made by the reforming or populist mayor John of Northampton (1381–3) to break the monopoly of the citizen fishmongers, in the interests of the citizens as consumers. It was claimed that the effect of the monopoly was to restrict supplies and raise prices.[58] Retail trade was opened to non-citizen fishmongers, who were encouraged to come to the city, but there was much discontent among the citizen fishmongers, and it is clear that they made things difficult for the foreign fishmongers. In 1382 a former Alderman was prosecuted for reviling the foreign fishmongers, and a proclamation of 1383 forbade anyone, citizen or stranger, to disturb, hinder or aggrieve any stranger victualler bringing and selling fish in the city, on pain of imprisonment.[59] But many of Northampton's measures roused strong opposition among the citizens whose interests were under attack, and his reforms did not long survive his mayoralty, which ended in October 1383. By 1399 the citizen fishmongers had gained confirmation of their old privileges, and the prohibition on foreigners selling retail was reaffirmed.[60] Henry IV, however, restored the foreign fishmongers' access to the markets, but the areas within which fish could be sold remained restricted.[61]

The main bone of contention in these disputes was the supply of fresh sea-fish to the city, and its sale in markets: the London fishmongers, who were large-scale dealers, regarded the Yarmouth and other sea-fishermen as rivals in the trade, and did their best to exclude them. They seem to have been less fearful of competition in the sale of salt and dried fish ('stockfish'), freshwater fish, and shellfish. The sellers of Thames or freshwater fish (which included eels) were regarded more as country producers were in other trades, encouraged to bring their catch and sell it themselves, but not allowed to sell it to dealers. In 1379 they were allowed to sell it at the Conduit (in Cheapside), by the church of St Margaret in Bridge Street, and by the church of St Mary Magdalen in Old Fish Street. In 1388 these standings seem to have been altered to Cheapside and Cornhill.[62]

In the thirteenth century shellfish (oysters, whelks, and mussels) were sold retail by those who had gathered them, from their boats; those unsold by noon could be bought in gross for resale in shops. By the fifteenth century both shellfish and salt fish could be sold by hawkers (*birlesters*) walking the streets; in 1588 seafish could also be hawked in the streets by fishwives and others, but not sold by them in markets.[63]

THE GRAIN AND MEAL MARKETS

In the late thirteenth century and the first half of the fourteenth, when the city's population was growing to its medieval maximum, regulation of the grain markets and the price of grain was an important concern of City government: meters of grain were appointed and sworn, and in 1344 regulations for the grain markets of Queenhithe, Billingsgate, Newgate pavement, and Gracechurch Street were proclaimed. The markets took place on Mondays, Wednesdays, and Fridays, opening at half prime in the waterside markets and prime in the street markets. Forestalling and regrating were forbidden, by definition if not by name, and no stranger was to sell by sample.[64] Grain came to London by land and by water, and each of the four markets was meant to be the centre for the produce from a particular direction. There is evidence for a complex supply system using the market at Henley for grain coming from the upper Thames valley, and landing it at Queenhithe.[65] Queenhithe and Billingsgate were also markets for salt in the medieval and early modern periods, a part of Queenhithe being known as the Saltwharf from the fourteenth century. Salt came to London by ship, imported from the bay of Bourgneuf in western France: Stow mentions the salt ships from the Bay unloading into lighters at Queenhithe.[66]

In the later middle ages, with the fall in population, there is less evidence of civic concern about the grain supply, though the building of Leadenhall as a granary in the 1440s probably reflects short-term anxiety. The grain market in Gracechurch Street seems to have moved inside Leadenhall when it opened.[67] By the sixteenth century, when population was again rising rapidly, the City was once again seriously concerned with its grain supply. The City authorities tried various ways of ensuring that there was a sufficient stock of grain held in the city; undoubtedly the threat of unrest driven by dearth of food in the city, of which they were conscious, was another aspect of the increasing problems London's food supply and market system were facing in the later sixteenth century.[68]

In the early sixteenth century the city asserted its claim to the open space or Romeland at Queenhithe and Billingsgate, where markets were held and (market) bells rung.[69] Both Queenhithe and Billingsgate had become to some extent general markets as well as grain and salt markets by the later sixteenth century. Billingsgate may by this date have been of less importance as a grain market: in 1580 persons were appointed to attend the city's meal markets at Leadenhall, Queeenhithe, and Southwark, but Billingsgate is not mentioned.[70] By this time it was evidently a place where fishwives could buy fish for resale, but it was not officially recognised as a fish market till the end of the seventeenth century.[71]

THE GENERAL MARKETS IN CHEAPSIDE, NEWGATE, CORNHILL AND LEADENHALL

The 'common markets' of Cheapside and Cornhill were where food of various kinds was sold: 'poultry wares', some meat, butter, cheese, herbs, roots, and fruits. Other goods also were sold here, Cheapside being lined with shops and selds from which goldsmiths' work, saddlery, woollen cloth, spices, silks and fine textiles were sold; Cornhill was known also as an old clothes market.[72] The street markets were primarily for Londoners to buy food for their own use. After a certain hour, however, traders could buy for resale: hucksters could buy cheese and butter after Prime, for resale by hawking but not in a market; denizen poulterers could buy poultry from foreign poulterers after Prime, as could cooks and regrators (hucksters or hawkers).[73]

The City seems to have been concerned to control the spread of these markets, both in time and place: in 1297 the 'noon fair' or afternoon market in Soper Lane (modern Queen Street) which had recently been established was forbidden, and in 1310 afternoon market trading in Cheapside was forbidden; only the 'common markets' of Cheapside and Cornhill were permitted, and they could only open from matins to noon.[74] Evening markets (*evechepynges*) in Cheap and Cornhill, held by old custom on feast-days, were recognised in 1393, but the time of closing, at the bell half an hour after sunset, was to be strictly observed; it is not clear if these were food markets.[75] By the early sixteenth century herb-wives, presumably country traders from the Cheapside market, were standing at the upper end of Soper Lane.[76]

It is not clear whether the general market that existed in the street inside Newgate by the late fourteenth century grew from the grain and meat markets there, or whether it should be seen as an extension of the Cheapside markets. Cheese was sold between the church of St Nicholas Shambles and Newgate in 1377;[77] foreign (non-citizen) poulterers coming to the city from the west stood on the pavement by the Grey Friars, while London poulterers stood before the church of St Nicholas Shambles. The latter rented plots in the street from the city, measuring 4½ ft to 6 ft in width, at 4*d*. per foot a year.[78] Citizen poulterers could also keep shops, of course, and the street of Poultry near the Stocks market contained several.[79]

The name 'Cornhill' in the fourteenth century denoted the street from the Stocks as far east as Lime Street, that is, including part of what is now known as Leadenhall Street. The 'Cornhill' market probably lay both west and east of the Bishopsgate Street-Gracechurch Street crossroads: the denizen poulterers had standing-places in front of St Michael Cornhill, and the foreign poulterers at the crossroads.[80] There is a reference in 1321 to foreign poulterers at Leadenhall (*la sale de plom*), though this was still a private house. Despite several references to the market 'at Leadenhall' in the fourteenth and early fifteenth centuries it is not clear that the market was held anywhere other than the street before the City built the granary and moved the market inside in 1445.[81] In the fifteenth century several citizen poulterers had shops in Cornhill/Leadenhall Street.[82] By the mid sixteenth century there was a general market in Gracechurch Street, probably an overflow from Leadenhall, which remained a meat, poultry, and grain market; there was also a general market in the street to the north of Leadenhall in 1598.[83]

Foreign cheesemongers and poulterers could only sell their wares in these markets.[84] In 1513 the foreign poulterers were enjoined to come directly to their accustomed markets of Leadenhall and the pavement by the Grey Friars, and to sell there only, and not in inns or any poulterer's house. No foreign poulterer was to sell in London any poultry bought by him from another foreign within seven miles of London.[85] Freemen poulterers were to sell only from their own houses and shops, at Leadenhall, Poultry, and Newgate Hill; in 1521 it was com-

plained that they were dressing their servants as husbandmen or country traders and sending them to stand in the (foreign) market of Cheapside.[86]

The commodities sold in these general markets were varied. Lists of prices for poultry include domestic poultry, coneys and rabbits, game, and waterfowl.[87] Some of these were alive, since poulterers were forbidden to take unsold 'stuff' away and 'herbage' it until the next market.[88] The poulterers also sold pigs (probably live), bacon, brawn, eggs, and butter.[89] The regulations of 1546, which confined the free and foreign butchers to St Nicholas Shambles, the Stocks, Eastcheap, and Leadenhall, confirmed nevertheless that all women and market folk and victuallers 'being no bochers' coming to the city with butter, cheese, fruit, etc., to sell in Newgate, Cheapside, and Gracechurch markets, might still sell 'veale, porke, bacon, sowse and such other lyke thyngs as in tymes paste hathe byn used and accustomed'.[90]

The ordinances of the cheesemongers, dating from 1377, show that they sold butter as well as cheese, but little is known of the varieties of these. In the fourteenth century Welsh traders brought a Welsh cheese called 'talgar'; in the early sixteenth century cheese and butter came from Suffolk and Essex.[91] The sale of vegetables (herbs and roots) in these markets is less well attested before the sixteenth century, though there are some references to the herb-wives of Cheapside and Soper Lane.[92] There were both free and foreign fruiterers, selling fruit from gardens in and around London, and imported from abroad. The foreign fruiterers could sell only in Cheapside, between the Standard and the Great Conduit, at Gracechurch, and by the Grey Friars at Newgate, but freemen and their servants could sell fruit anywhere. In 1463 the market days for the foreign fruiterers were Mondays, Wednesdays, and Fridays, before noon, but in 1465 Saturday was added to these.[93]

SMITHFIELD

The market here for live animals, including horses, was noted by FitzStephen in the later twelfth century; cows, pigs, oxen and horses were sold there in the fourteenth century.[94] As with the other markets, the proper places for different traders to stand were defined: in 1379 the freemen drovers selling cattle were to stand between Long Lane and the street coming from

Aldersgate, those selling swine near to St Bartholomew's Hospital. The foreign drovers could sell anywhere within the field of Smithfield except in those two places.[95]

In 1527 penalties were prescribed for forestalling various goods including livestock (oxen, kine, calves, sheep, lambs, and hogs) before they came to the market. At the same time it was reiterated that no foreign could buy and sell livestock from any other foreign except at Smithfield market, that is on Wednesdays and Fridays between eleven and one o'clock; and all sales of horses were to take place in the open market place and not in stables or houses.[96]

The market at Smithfield was adjacent to the site of St Bartholomew's Fair, held in August, primarily for cloth and other merchandise. The fair dated from the early eleventh century, and was the cause of some dissension between the City and St Bartholomew's Priory, until they agreed to run it jointly from the mid fifteenth century.[97]

THE MARKETS BY THE LATE SIXTEENTH CENTURY

By the late sixteenth century the population of London was nearing 200,000, and this had greatly increased the pressure on the traditional markets, as well as changing the scope and extent of the capital's food supply network.[98] The City seems to have found it more and more difficult to control the markets: as well as the increasing problems of overcrowding and lack of accommodation, as the markets spilled over in time and space from their accustomed limits, it had to cope with national changes in the way in which food was marketed. As a result of the growth of population in the country as a whole, it was hardly possible for the first producers to continue to market their own produce in person, and the growth of middlemen, contracts, and 'private marketing' in this period changed the context in which the London markets functioned. In their attempts to enforce regulations prohibiting forestalling and engrossing, the authorities seem to have tried, without success, to resist these general changes.[99] Hugh Alley's *Caveat* was itself an unofficial response to the problems of the markets and the enforcement of regulations, and fits into a general context of concern and schemes for reform of the organisation of marketing in London.[100]

The City authorities were also concerned with how the increased food needs of the capital were to be met, and some of the market regulation of this period seems to spring from this consciousness. A sense of urgency in the city was perhaps sharpened by the harvest failures and dearth of the mid-1590s, when the food supply of London seemed to be in danger (though in fact it never failed) and the offences against fair market practice, against which Alley rails, were perhaps particularly noticeable.[101] The City had some success in tackling the problems of market accommodation, asserting its right to the open land at Billingsgate in 1523–5 and again in 1544, partly paving Smithfield market in 1567, and repaving 'market hill' in Newgate Street in 1588. It built new market houses at Newgate in 1547, at Queenhithe in 1564–6, and enlarged both in the 1590s. A market house for grain was built in Southwark in the later sixteenth century (probably before 1577), and enlarged in 1606. The possibility of setting up a new meal market near Bishopsgate was investigated in 1592; the desirability of improved accommodation for the meal-sellers at Leadenhall was recognised in 1592 and 1595, though other interests made this hard to achieve. The Bishopsgate market, for malt and yarn, was authorised and built in 1599, and from 1600 was ordered to be used as a meal market.[102] It is significant that most of this building activity concerned the grain or meal markets, reflecting the City's acute concern with its grain supply in these years.

A new 'city' market was added in the sixteenth century, when the existing market in Southwark came fully under the City's control in 1550. There had been a weekly market here since the fifteenth century at least, but the City's acquisition of extensive rights in the Borough included full jurisdiction of and tolls from the market, which was thereafter held on four days a week (Monday, Wednesday, Friday, and Saturday).[103]

In the sixteenth century market days and hours were being extended, both officially and unofficially, from medieval custom. By 1551 the Shambles, the Stocks, and Eastcheap meat markets seem to have been open six days a week, from 6 a.m. until 11, and from 1 p.m. until 5; in 1546 the foreign butchers were only allowed to sell in Leadenhall, on Wednesdays and Saturdays, until noon, but from 1553 were allowed to sell in the afternoons of their market days as well.[104] In 1581 an order stated that the Cheapside market should close within half an hour of the ringing of the bell at noon, but by 1592 the inhabitants of the street were complaining that the market was kept on the Sabbath and every other day from morning till 9 o'clock at night, sometimes by candlelight.[105] In 1613 an extra day (Monday) was granted for Smithfield market, specifically because the growth of population had made it impossible for the city to be sufficiently served by the present two market days.[106]

Sunday trading seems in fact to have been common, though the City tried to limit it. In 1561 herbwives and others were forbidden to sell herbs or flowers in the markets or streets on Sundays. In 1588 the sale of milk, herbs, flowers and roots on Sundays was restricted to before 7 a.m. (8 a.m. in winter); fruit could not be sold on Sundays except for 'timely fruits', cherries, strawberries, etc., which might be sold in season by basketmen walking the streets. This contrasts with the four days allowed to the foreign fruiterers in the fifteenth century.[107]

The pressure on market space and time was perhaps also responsible for the tendency for traders to try and sell in the 'wrong' markets. In 1521 the citizen poulterers were accused of encroaching on the country traders' position in the Cheapside market.[108] In the 1540s free and foreign butchers were forbidden to sell flesh in the general markets, which suggests they had been doing so; a report on the state of the markets in 1588 ordered that no butcher should sell in the streets if there was room at Leadenhall or in the Greenyard adjoining it.[109] The same report also recommended that goods such as linen cloth, pots, and glasses should only be sold in shops and warehouses, and not in the markets, which were for the sale of 'victuals, herbs, and other things mentioned'. Nor were salted or barrelled butter, white or red herring, to be resold there; and the fishwives and other hucksters were to walk the streets to sell, and not stand in the marketplaces.[110]

As a result of the report on the markets in 1588, the City tried to improve the organisation of the market in Cheapside, placing foreign victuallers between the Cross and the Great Conduit, and the sellers of flowers, herbs, roots, and seeds between the Cross and the Little Conduit, at the west end. The flower-sellers were to stand on the south side of the channel, the others on the north. No root-seller was to have more than three baskets at a time, and the washing of vegetables in the street was forbidden.[111] Nevertheless by 1592 the inhabitants of Cheapside were complaining of congestion in the street, of the

cost of clearing the rubbish, which was borne by the parishes, and of the illegal hours at which the market remained open.[112]

It was more difficult, however, to control market practices, especially those which reflected changes in marketing patterns generally. From the reign of Henry VIII the City tried repeatedly to prevent forestalling and private selling, whether of livestock, poultry or other foodstuffs.[113] Concluding that the victualling Companies were failing to supervise the markets in their own goods adequately and control prices in the interests of the consumers, it assigned members of other Companies to attend the markets: members of the Drapers', Grocers', Mercers', and Goldsmiths' Companies, in rotation, to the flesh markets in 1534; others to the fish markets in 1543; members of the twelve great Livery Companies to the meal markets in 1580.[114] Prosecutions recorded in the City's Book of Fines (probably only the tip of the iceberg) suggest that regrating was common in the 1580s and 1590s; several persistent offenders are noted.[115] There was also, clearly, an increasing tendency to sell outwith the market system altogether; the problem of innholders 'harbouring' meal was mentioned in connection with the establishment of the Bishopsgate market, as an argument for increasing the City's provision of markets.[116]

This evidence for the greater strain London's market system was under in the late sixteenth century, and the endeavours of the City to cope with changed marketing conditions and new pressures, form the background to Alley's *Caveat* of 1598 and his proposals for reform of the market system.

NOTES

[1] Betty R. Masters, *The public markets of the City of London surveyed by William Leybourn in 1677* (LTS, 1974), pp. 13–20.
[2] Harben, pp. 492–3; A. J. Robertson, *Laws of the kings of England from Edmund to Henry I* (1925), p. 71.
[3] E. Ekwall, *Street-names of the City of London* (1954), pp. 182–5.
[4] Ibid., pp. 72, 76, 103, 107.
[5] Cf. Derek Keene and Vanessa Harding, *Survey of documentary sources for property holding in London before the Great Fire* (LRS 22, 1985), no. 70 and index; Harben, pp. 448–9. It is uncertain whether the earlier *veteri Piscaria* and *vico Piscario* Harben mentions refer to the Cheapside fish market or that in Old Fish Street.
[6] See below, p. 9; *Lib. Alb.*, i, p. 433.
[7] Stow, ii, p. 223; see below.
[8] E.g. *Lib. Cust.*, i, pp. 61–3; *Memorials*, pp. 166, 580–1, 643.

⁹ Cronica Maiorum et Vicecomitum Londoniarum, printed as *De Antiquis Legibus Liber*, ed. T. Stapleton (Camden Society 34, 1846), p. 164; *Rotuli Hundredorum* (Record Commission, 1812), i, pp. 403, 415, 428. I owe these references and those in notes 10 and 19 to Derek Keene Director of the Social and Economic Study of Medieval London.

¹⁰ Annales Londonienses, printed as *Chronicles of the reigns of Edward I and Edward II*, ed. W. Stubbs (Rolls Series 76, 1882–3), i, p. 90.

¹¹ CLRO, Husting Roll (Deeds), 14 (76).

¹² Ibid.

¹³ CLRO, Bridge House Deeds F 48.

¹⁴ *CLBF*, p. 123.

¹⁵ Stow, i, p. 226; *Great Chronicle of London*, ed. A. H. Thomas and I. D. Thornley (1938, repr. 1983), p. 88; see below, p. 89.

¹⁶ *Memorials*, p. 73; see below, p. 87–8.

¹⁷ *Memorials*, pp. 222–3.

¹⁸ Harben, pp. 343–5; A. H. Thomas, 'Notes on the history of the Leadenhall, 1195–1488', *LTR* 13 (1923), pp. 1–22; CLRO, Journal 5, ff. 114, 326. The Department of Urban Archaeology of the Museum of London has recently excavated part of the fifteenth-century building and graphically reconstructed its appearance.

¹⁹ CLRO, Bridge House Small Register, f. 83; *CLBH*, p. 145.

²⁰ Harben, pp. 343–5, citing *Calendar of Patent Rolls, 1461–7*, p. 285, and *CLBL*, p. 36; Masters, *Public Markets . . . surveyed by William Leybourn*, pp. 20–2; Thomas, 'Leadenhall', pp. 20–2.

²¹ H. M. Chew and M. Weinbaum (ed.), *The London Eyre of 1244* (LRS 6, 1970), no. 486.

²² T. Madox, *History of the Exchequer* (London 1711), i, p. 534n; PRO, SC6/917/1. I owe the first of these references and discussion of the point to Derek Keene.

²³ *Lib. Alb.*, i, p. 136, cap. 90; *Lib. Cust.*, i, pp. 46–7; Chew and Weinbaum, *London Eyre of 1244*, nos. 248–68; *CLBG*, pp. 314–15.

²⁴ *Lib. Alb.*, i, pp. 162–71, cap. 484; for rents taken for standings in Cheapside cf. *CPMR 1458–1482*, pp. 118–19 (1478), and CLRO, Rep. 23, ff. 383–4 (1595). For the ban on other markets see *Lib. Alb.*, i, p. 147, cap. 204.

²⁵ G. A. Williams, *Medieval London, from Commune to Capital* (1963), pp. 44–8; *Lib. Alb.*, i, pp. 127–8, caps. 157–61, 166; ibid. pp. 146–52, caps. 429, 434, 471.

²⁶ E.g. CLRO, Liber Horn, flyleaf.

²⁷ *Lib. Alb.*, i, pp. 263–4, 275; *Memorials, passim*; cf. e.g. *CLBG*, pp. 33, 198; *CEMCR*, pp. 157–8; *CPMR 1413–37*, pp. 122, 136, 138, 151. For the prosecution of these offences in the sixteenth century, see below, p. 22–5.

²⁸ *Lib. Alb.*, i, p. 357 (*regraterissis* of bread); *Memorials*, p. 508. 'Huckster' also originally denoted a female trader: *OED*.

²⁹ CLRO, Rep. 21, f. 543v.

³⁰ *CLBG*, pp. 33; *Memorials*, pp. 141–2, 580–1.

³¹ *Lib. Alb.*, i, pp. 261–3; *CPMR 1323–64*, pp. 95n., 119, 193.

³² *Lib. Alb.*, i, pp. 599–610; *Memorials, passim*. As an example: Margery Hove, *fisshwyfe*, was sentenced in 1372 to the thew (the pillory for women) for offering rotten sole for sale at the Stocks. The fish was to be burnt before her: *Memorials*, p. 367.

³³ *Calendar of Close Rolls, 1364–8*, p. 74; *Memorials*, pp. 435–6.

³⁴ *Memorials*, pp. 598–9.

³⁵ C. L. Kingsford (ed.), *Chronicles of London* (1905, repr. 1977), p. 156; Caroline M. Barron, 'The government of London and its relations with the crown, 1400–1450' (unpublished London Ph.D. thesis, 1970), pp. 251–2; CLRO, Rep. 21, f. 542v.

³⁶ *CLBF*, p. 101. The canonical hours began with 'matins' at about midnight, and 'prime' at 6 a.m. or sunrise: *OED*, and C. R. Cheney, *Handbook of dates for students of English history* (Royal Historical Society, 1978), p. 9. Their secular interpretation is less clear, however; it seems improbable that the markets opened in the middle of the night.

³⁷ *Memorials*, pp. 220–1, 300, 405–7; *CLBH*, p. 214; CLRO, Journal 11, f. 169.

³⁸ *CLBL*, pp. 30–4, 57.

³⁹ CLRO, Bridge House, Bridgewardens Account Rolls 1381–1400, *passim*; *Memorials*, p. 426.

⁴⁰ Stow, ii, p. 223; CLRO, Letterbook O, f. 35v.

⁴¹ Barron, thesis, pp. 239–40, 250, 252; *Memorials*, pp. 253–8 (wages and prices, 1350), 312, 426, 432, 458, 580–1, 643, 666.

⁴² For the assize of bread, see Barron, thesis, pp. 239–42, and *Lib. Alb.*, i, pp. 349–58.

⁴³ *Memorials*, p. 643; CLRO, Rep. 10, ff. 331v–334.

⁴⁴ Barron, thesis, pp. 225, 227, 229, 230. Cf. *CLBD*, p. 7 (oath of the bailiffs of Queenhithe and Billingsgate).

⁴⁵ Barron, thesis, pp. 249–51; P. E. Jones, *The Butchers of London* (1976), pp. 77–84.

⁴⁶ Barron, thesis, p. 239; S. Thrupp, *A short history of the Worshipful Company of Bakers of London* (1933), pp. 56–64; *Lib. Alb.*, i, pp. 264–5, 349–58; *Memorials*, pp. 38–9, 119, 323–4; *CLBL*, pp. 294–5, 301, 305–6.

⁴⁷ *Memorials*, pp. 347–8 (ale); ibid., pp. 181–3, 213 (wine); *CLBH*, pp. 214–15 (ale); *Memorials*, pp. 257, 266, 426, 432, 438, 448 (cooks, pastelers, and piebakers).

⁴⁸ Barron, thesis, p. 256.

⁴⁹ Masters, *Public markets . . . surveyed by William Leybourn*, p. 14; Jones, *Butchers*, especially pp. 77–87.

⁵⁰ Jones, *Butchers*, pp. 76–81; cf. *Memorials*, pp. 356–8.

⁵¹ See above, p. 4. .

⁵² In 1283, when the Stocks market was leased, it was stated that no other butchers' stalls would be permitted except in Eastcheap and near St Nicholas (Shambles): CLRO, Husting Roll (Deeds) 14(76). In 1408 a proclamation again forbade the sale of flesh except at the Stocks, the butchery in Eastcheap, and the butchery at St Nicholas *Flesshammes*: *CLBI*, p. 61.

⁵³ Jones, *Butchers*, pp. 89–90; CLRO, Letterbook, Q, f. 186; Rep. 11, f. 280 [now f. 257].

⁵⁴ *Memorials*, p. 599; CLRO, Journal 11, f. 172v; Jones, *Butchers*, p. 76. For the possible origin of the 'middle row' in the Shambles, see above, p. 4.

⁵⁵ Jones, *Butchers*, p. 73; *Analytical Index to the series of records known as the Remembrancia . . . 1579–1664* (1878), 202, II.55.

⁵⁶ *Lib. Cust.*, i, pp. 385–406.

⁵⁷ *CLBG*, p. 77; *Lib. Cust.*, i, pp. 393, 404. Freshwater and shell-fish could be bought from the boats in which it was brought: see below.

[58] Ruth Bird, *The turbulent London of Richard II* (1949), pp. 63–85; *Memorials*, pp. 467–72, 481–2.

[59] *Memorials*, pp. 467–70, 473–4, 481–2.

[60] Bird, *Turbulent London*, pp. 112–13; *Memorials*, p. 494; *CLBH*, pp. 447–8.

[61] Barron, thesis, p. 248; *Memorials*, p. 599. Fish marketing in London at a later period is discussed in W. M. Stern, 'Fish marketing in London in the first half of the eighteenth century', in D. C. Coleman and A. H. John (ed.), *Trade, Government and Society in pre-Industrial England: essays presented to F. J. Fisher* (1976), pp. 68–77.

[62] *Memorials*, pp. 436, 508–9; *CLBH*, p. 373; *CPMR 1381–1412*, p. 220. A list of prices for freshwater fish in 1543 named roach, dace, flounders, lampreys, smelts, gudgeon, eels of various kinds and sizes, and shrimps: CLRO, Rep. 10, f. 314.

[63] *Lib. Alb.*, i, pp. 381–2; *Memorials*, p. 508; CLRO, Rep. 21, f. 544,

[64] *CLBF*, pp. 100–1; see n. 36.

[65] *Lib. Alb.*, i, p. 433; *CLBG*, p. 330; V. A. Harding, 'The Port of London in the fourteenth century, its topography, administration, and trade' (unpublished Ph.D. thesis, St Andrews 1983), p. 40.

[66] Harding, thesis, pp. 39–42; Stow, ii, p. 10.

[67] Above, p. 4; Barron, thesis, pp. 246–7, 413–15.

[68] N. S. B. Gras, *The evolution of the English corn market from the twelfth to the eighteenth century* (Harvard, 1915), pp. 77–94; S. Rappaport, 'Social structure and mobility in sixteenth-century London', part I, *London Journal* 9 (1983), pp. 125–31; M J. Power, 'London and the control of the 'crisis' of the 1590s', *History* 70 (1985), pp. 372–5.

[69] CCPR Billingsgate.

[70] CLRO, Journal 21, f. 84; below, p. 12.

[71] CLRO, Rep. 21, f. 543v; Stern, 'Fish marketing', pp. 71–2.

[72] Derek Keene, *Cheapside before the Great Fire* (ESRC pamphlet, 1985), pp. 12–17; *Lib. Cust.*, i, p. 426. See also the fifteenth century poem 'London Lickpenny', printed in (for example) Everyman's Library, *The Golden Treasury of Longer Poems* (repr. 1954), pp. 53–6.

[73] *Memorials*, pp. 220–1, 405–7; *CLBG*, p. 271. Cf. CLRO, Journal 11, f. 169 (1513).

[74] *CLBB*, p. 236; *CLBD*, p. 229; *Lib. Cust.*, i, p. 426.

[75] *Memorials*, pp. 532–4.

[76] Derek Keene and Vanessa Harding, *Historical Gazetteer of London before the Great Fire*, i, Cheapside, 145/8, 145/30; Stow, i, p. 268.

[77] *Memorials*, p. 405

[78] *CLBG*, pp. 271, 314–15; cf. *Memorials*, pp. 298–300, 389.

[79] *Memorials*, p. 222; CLRO, Journal 12, f. 118r–v; information from Derek Keene.

[80] *CLBG*, p. 271; *Memorials*, pp. 298–300, 389.

[81] Harben, pp. 343–5; A. H. Thomas, 'Notes on the history of the Leadenhall, 1195–1488', *LTR* 13 (1923), pp. 1–22; *Lib. Cust.*, i, p. 305; *Memorials*, pp. 405–7. In March 1455 Common Council ordered that from Easter next the common market of poultry, victuals, grain, eggs, butter, and cheese, lately held at (*apud*) Leadenhall, was to be held within (*infra*) the new granary constructed there by Simon Eyre: CLRO, Journal 5, f. 235.

[82] Vanessa Harding and Priscilla Metcalf, *Lloyd's at home, the background and the buildings* (1986), pp. 32–3.

[83] CLRO, Letterbook Q, f. 186; Rep. 11, f. 490v; see below, p. 87–8.

[84] *Memorials*, pp. 405–7; cf. *CLBG*, p. 271; *Memorials*, pp. 298–300.

[85] CLRO, Journal 11, f. 169

[86] CLRO, Journal 12, f. 118r–v.

[87] *Memorials*, p. 312 (mentioning geese, capons, hens, rabbits, river mallard, teal, larks, snipe, woodcock, partridge, pheasant); CLRO, Journal 11, f. 27 (also mentions swans, cranes, bustards, herons, shoveler, bittern, stork, rabbit 'runners' and 'suckers', plover, quail, and curlew); ibid., f. 169.

[88] Ordinances of the Poulters, CLRO, Rep. 10, ff. 331v–334. Citizens could keep hens and capons at home, but swans and geese could only be kept in the open spaces by London Wall, because of the smell: CLRO, Journal 11, f. 169.

[89] CLRO, Journal 11, f. 169.

[90] CLRO, Letterbook Q, f. 186. 'Sowse' seems to have been some kind of salted or spiced meat product, perhaps like brawn; cf. *OED*.

[91] *Memorials*, pp. 405–7 (Riley suggests Talgarth fair as the origin of 'talgar' cheese); CLRO, Letterbook Q, f. 86v; F. J. Fisher,' The development of the London food market, 1540–1640', *Economic History Review* 5 (1934–5), pp. 48, 51.

[92] Keene and Harding, *Historical Gazetteer of London before the Great Fire*, i, Cheapside, 145/8, 145/30.

[93] *CEMCR*, pp. 137–8; *CPMR* 1458–82, pp. 118–19; *CLBL*, pp. 30–4, 57, 234. For imports of fruit and vegetables from abroad in the fourteenth century, see Harding, thesis, pp. 218–221.

[94] Stow, ii, p. 223; *CEMCR*, pp. 94, 173; *CPMR 1323–64*, pp. 217, 242.

[95] *Memorials*, pp. 435–6.

[96] CLRO, Letterbook O, f. 35v.

[97] Harben, p. 50; Barron, thesis, p. 326; cf. Stow, ii, p. 27.

[98] The approximate figure of 200,000 for the population of the metropolis c.1600 is offered both by I. Sutherland, 'When was the Great Plague? Mortality in London, 1563 to 1665', in D. V. Glass and R. Revelle (ed.), *Population and social change* (1972), pp. 287–320, and by B. Shearer and R. Finlay, 'Population growth and suburban expansion', in A. L. Beier and R. Finlay (ed.) *London 1500–1700, The Making of the metropolis* (1986), pp. 37–59.

[99] These changes are discussed in F. J. Fisher, 'The development of the London food market 1540–1640', *Economic History Review* 5 (1934–5), pp. 46–64; A. Everitt, 'The marketing of agricultural produce', in Joan Thirsk (ed.), *The Agrarian History of England and Wales*, iv, *1500–1640*, pp. 466–592; P. V. McGrath, The marketing of food, fodder, and livestock in the London area in the seventeenth century (unpublished London M.A. thesis, 1948).

[100] See below, pp. 22–7.

[101] Below, p. 25; cf. M. J. Power, 'London and the control of the 'crisis' of the 1590s', *History* 70 (1985), pp. 372–5.

[102] See below, pp. 84, 92, 94, 96–7; CCPR Billingsgate, Leadenhall, Newgate market, Queenhithe. For the Bishopsgate market, see CLRO, Rep. 24, f. 411; Rep. 25, ff. 105, 147v; Journal 25, ff. 220v–221.

[103] David J. Johnson, *Southwark and the City* (1969), pp. 128, 305; CCPR Southwark; see below, pp. 96–7.

[104] CLRO, Letterbook Q, ff. 174, 186; Rep. 11 f. 72r–v [now f. 70]; Rep. 12 (2), f. 320.

[105] CLRO, Rep. 20, f. 237v; Rep. 22, ff. 408v–409.

[106] CLRO, Letterbook EE, ff. 179v–180.

[107] CLRO, Letterbook T, f. 46v; Rep. 21, ff. 542–543v; *CLBL*, p. 57.

[108] CLRO, Journal 12, f. 118r–v.

[109] CLRO, Letterbook Q, ff. 174, 186; Rep. 21, f. 543v.

[110] CLRO, Rep. 21, ff. 543–4.

[111] Ibid., ff. 542v–543.

[112] CLRO, Rep. 22, ff. 408v–409.

[113] E.g. CLRO, Letterbook O, f. 35v; Rep. 10, ff. 331v–334.

[114] CLRO, Rep. 9, ff. 64v–65; Rep. 10, 315; Rep. 11, f. 72 [now f. 70]; Journal 21, f. 84.

[115] CLRO, Book of Fines, 1517–1628, ff. 225–32; see below, p. 23.

[116] CLRO, Journal 25, ff. 220v–221.

HUGH ALLEY, LAW ENFORCEMENT, AND MARKET REGULATION IN THE LATER SIXTEENTH CENTURY

What are those that stand so close
At the street corner, pricking up their noses, like rich men's dogs
When the first course goes in? By the mass, promoters![1]

The drawings reproduced in this volume were conceived as part of a campaign by the professional Westminster informer, Hugh Alley, to establish himself as an enforcer of market regulations in the city of London. Alley presented his *Caveat* to the lord mayor, Sir Richard Saltonstall in April 1598, shortly after receiving the freedom of the city by redemption at the request of Lord Treasurer Burghley.[2] The *Caveat* records that its author had made careful observation of the markets, and briefly points to the abuses of hawkers who bought up produce for resale out of the markets and so contributed to increasing prices. But the work contains no specific proposals for reform; rather Alley refers vaguely to his hope to stir up better consciences among offenders by his denunciation of abuses. The rather disinterested tone of the work, however, should be taken with a pinch of salt. By the beginning of 1599 he clearly had more specific proposals, for in February, and again in July, committees of the Court of Aldermen were considering Alley's proposals for the reformation of market abuses.[3] On 25 September the aldermen ordered that Alley was to oversee the markets to prevent hucksters from engrossing victuals for resale.[4] This arrangement was formalised by Common Council on 4 February 1600 in an act appointing four overseers of the markets, to each of whom was appointed a circuit among the markets.[5]

The act opened with a ringing denunciation of the offenders identified in the *Caveat*:

> Forasmuch as divers and sundrye forreyners Inmates undersitters and others idle and evill disposed persones framing themselves to leade a more easie lyfe then by labor, have of long tyme and yet daylye doe use and frequent the markettes of this Citie, To regrate, forestall and ingrosse all kind of victuall, fruictes, and all other thinges of lyke nature coming and being to and in the same markettes, whereby all the best and chief thinges are not onely by the forenamed evill disposed persones comonly called hucksters hawkers haglers and wanderers up and downe the streetes of the same markettes bought up before anie the good Citizens of this Citie can come by the same, To the greate enhauncing of the pryce, And hinderaunce and disproffite of the inhabitauntes of the sayd citie which is lyke to continue and encrease, if some good lawe be not made to redresse the same . . .

The overseers were instructed to be present in the markets throughout the market time, ringing the bell at the close of trading, and taking care to ensure that all the market people promptly departed. They were to keep registers of trading offences which were to be presented each week to the alderman or the deputy of the ward in which the market was located, and abstracts were to be prepared for the Lord Mayor every three months. The attention of the overseers was drawn particularly to traders who kept their products away from public view, presumably because of some precontract with a hawker. Any goods found to be hidden in this way were to be sold at prices thought fit by the overseers subject to the consent of the owner. But the harshest penalties were reserved for the hawkers themselves: any produce forestalled, regrated, or engrossed was to be seized as forfeit by the overseers, half the forfeitures going to the City Chamber and the other half to the presenting officers.[6]

We know very little about how Alley's scheme operated in practice. The act did make provision for the bringing of information in the Mayor's Court against offenders, but there are none extant in the admittedly patchy records of this court. Informations may not have been necessary in all cases however as the act seems to have envisaged that the overseers should hold summary powers. Such summary jurisdiction was held by other relatively lowly City officials: John Stow's account of his service as one of the four annually elected surveyors of beer shows the surveyors ordering alehouse keepers with unlawful measures to send beer into the hospitals to atone for their offences.[7] More problematic is the relative absence of fines received from the overseers in the City's Book of Fines, in which the Chamberlain, who was entitled to a portion of the forfeitures under the 1600 act, recorded receipts of fines for the breach of City trading regulations. The Book of Fines in fact only records one fine explicitly received from the overseers: in June 1600 20s. was received from Thomas Atkins, fishmonger for forestalling 200 codfish before they came to market at Billingsgate.[8] However, the absence of fines should not be taken as a sign of inactivity; rather it is probable that the Chamber waived its claim, or alternatively that the Chamberlain recorded receipts from the overseers separately.[9] The aldermen ordered a payment of £10 to the overseers in January 1601 for their services, and a further £28 followed in June.[10] It seems that the registers of markets offences were kept, for these were probably the 'divers bookes rolles & wrytinges which he hathe written and taken within this Citty sithence the tyme he was first appointed ... to be one of the overseers', which Alley was instructed to deliver to the Chamberlain.[11] Other groups in city society with an interest in the markets were impressed with Alley, for the ruling assistants of the Fishmongers' Company were prepared to put some of their company's money behind the scheme, rewarding Alley with 20s. for his pains in removing fishwives from the markets.[12]

In the face of this evidence for the conscientious discharge of their duties, the reasons for Common Council's decision to abandon the regulation of the markets through the overseers in January 1602 become all the more puzzling. Unfortunately the order of Common Council gives no hint of the explanation.[13] There are several possibilities. First, the summary powers wielded by the overseers may have proved controversial, particularly if any of the incumbents fell prey to the easy temptations to sharp practice. Certainly it was common for

powers of the type exercised by the overseers to be resisted by harassing the officials concerned by means of counter-litigation.[14] Secondly, the fact that the overseers were intruding on the responsibilities of existing officers, in particular of the officers of the mayor's household, may have led them into clashes with these officers. The act of February 1600 provided that the registers of offences kept by the overseers should be supplemented by weekly reports to the mayor from the existing officials. It is as though the two groups of officials were being used as checks on each other's diligence. Unfortunately, there is no positive evidence that the officers of the mayor's household resented the intrusion on their sphere, although one might reasonably expect friction given that the profits of office were at stake.[15] A third possibility is that at a time when the City was subject to heavy financial demands from the Crown, the City Chamber may have felt the cost of supporting the overseers an unnecessary extravagance: including the cost of paying Alley's creditors, the scheme had cost the Chamber at least £50. Perhaps their impact on the markets was not felt to justify expenditure of this level. It is, of course, perfectly reasonable to suppose that the scheme was brought down by a combination of these factors.

It is the purpose of this part of the introduction to set the initiative of 1599–1602 in the context of the problems of law enforcement in general, and market regulation in particular, in the later sixteenth century. Because Alley worked as a professional informer in the Court of Exchequer before beginning his city career, it is possible through an examination of his activities to attempt some comparison of law enforcement in central and local jurisdictions. Both the Queen's Council, and to a lesser extent, the City Corporation were forced to acknowledge their dependence on enforcement through informer actions, whether in the Exchequer or the Mayor's Court, by private individuals whose interest in securing the enforcement of the law was tempered by an interest in making a profit out of infractions through their portion of the penalties. The crucial questions are those of control. How far did informer sponsored law enforcement reflect the priorities of the Council and the City Corporation rather than the relative ease with which the informer could make a profit out of a particular offence? How much control over potential abuses by the informer did the relevant authorities exercise? The first section of this discussion outlines the known facts about Alley's life; the second deals with his career as Exchequer informer; and the third discusses market regulation in Elizabethan London, and establishes a context for Alley's initiative.

THE CAREER OF HUGH ALLEY

Hugh Alley was born in the parish of St Margaret Westminster in October 1556, the first-born son of Simon Alley and Joanne Wyatt.[16] The family were long-term residents of the parish. Hugh's grandfather, John, a collar maker, died there in 1554;[17] Simon Alley, a rochet-maker by occupation, leased two tenements in the Almonry from the Dean and Chapter from 1565, renewing the lease in 1604.[18] Although he does not appear to have held major office in the parish, Simon enjoyed some standing there, auditing the churchwardens' accounts in 1580 and 1582.[19] But thereafter his fortunes appear to have decayed. His poor rate assessment, 2*d.* per week in 1582, fell to 1*d.* per week in 1586, and 6*d.* per quarter in 1587.[20] From August 1593 until his death in 1607 he served the lowly position of sexton in St Margaret's.[21] The bond between Simon and his son was probably close. Hugh was also resident in the parish for most of his life, only moving to St Botolph Aldgate in 1601, and then only because of his recently acquired responsibilities in the city.[22] He actually leased property next door to his father, and although Hugh predeceased Simon in December 1602, it was for Hugh's son, Edward, that Simon reserved his most affectionate words in his will, leaving him the lease of his house 'in regarde of his kynde usage of him and dutiefulness towards him according to his abilitie'.[23]

Hugh did not follow his family into the clothing trades. When he first surfaces in the documents in 1574 at the tender age of eighteen, it is in his capacity as a newly appointed clerk on the royal building works on a wage of 12*d.* per day. For the next eight years the accounts generally record payments to him at this rate for about 270 days each year. His duties are variously described as 'overseing the woorkemen and Laborors & keaping the cheque booke', 'engrossinge the paye and signed bookes', 'taking noate of the Receipte & delyverie of the Emptions'. This work took him around the various royal palaces which circled London: he is recorded as serving at Whitehall, St James's, Greenwich, Oatlands, Hampton Court,

and Richmond. The personnel of the royal works were, as Julia Merritt is demonstrating, a pervasive force in the local government of Westminster, and would have brought Alley valuable contacts and patronage, possibly even within the Exchequer.[24]

There is little indication of the means by which Alley made a living between 1582, the date his name disappears from the works accounts, and 1590, the date when he first appeared before the Barons of the Exchequer with informations for infringements of penal statutes. It is likely that he exploited his clerical skills for a local clientele: the churchwardens' accounts of St Margaret's record payments to him for providing writing materials and for binding the accounts. Furthermore the accounts were actually drawn up at Alley's house in 1598.[25] Almost as soon as he obtained the freedom of the Plaisterers' Company in 1597, the company was drawing on his clerical services in their parliamentary campaign against the Painters: the accounts record numerous payments to him 'for writings touching parliament'.[26]

There is a tantalising hint that Alley may have been involved in market regulation within Westminster long before his appointment in the city. The churchwardens' accounts for 1588–89 record a payment of 18*s.* to Alley for twelve new stamps to mark weights for the parish.[27] This was part of the parish response to a recent royal proclamation of December 1587, which instructed the officers of market towns to fetch copies of the recently re-established standard weights from the Exchequer, by which other weights were to be tested. From Michaelmas 1588 no weights were to be used which failed to comply with the Exchequer standards, and local officials were instructed to examine weights periodically, and to deface any found defective. Authorised weights were to be stamped.[28] It therefore looks as if Alley had been appointed to assay weights within Westminster, applying his stamps to those which accorded with the Exchequer standards.

Because of the formality of his appearances in the documents — there is no will and he has left no testimony more personal than the *Caveat* — it is difficult to say much about Hugh's personality. But bumptious and meddlesome are the adjectives which most readily come to mind. His neighbours in Westminster certainly regarded him potentially meddlesome. When his father was appointed sexton in 1593 the parish vestry made it a condition of his appointment that he should not 'permitt his son hewgh Alley in any wise to entermeadle or deale in the same office'.[29] Ever a busybody, he was always on the lookout for some new field for the exercise of his reformist inclinations. Nor was he easily put down. When imprisoned in one of the City's Counters for debt, he bounced back with a petition to the aldermen concerning abuses in the administration of the prisons.[30] He was clearly a lower class denizen of that underworld of projectors and Sir Politic Would-Bes, fertile with schemes purportedly combining private profit and the interests of the commonweal, which so thrived at the turn of the century.

HUGH ALLEY AND EXCHEQUER INFORMING

The absence of a professional police force left the Tudors dependent upon private enterprise for the enforcement of much of their legislation. The private citizen was encouraged to enforce the law by the prospect of a portion of the forfeiture in the event of a successful prosecution. Thus most of the Tudor legislation affecting the economy allowed the informer against the offence half of the forfeiture recovered from the defendant. Informations could be brought in any court of record, but they were most regularly brought to the attention of the Barons of the Exchequer court at Westminster. The informer would give details of the offence he had uncovered to one of the Remembrancer's clerks who would engross a summary on the parchment Memoranda Rolls. The parchment bill was shown to the Barons who would authorise process to be sued out once the informer had sworn to the truth of his allegation.[31]

Alley first appears as an Exchequer informer in Michaelmas term of 1590 when he brought informations concerning an illegal enclosure in Leicestershire, the use of wood in iron manufacture by five Sussex men, and the cutting of trees in barking time also in Sussex.[32] Until 1598 he continued to bring a stream of informations on a variety of penal statutes: in 1594 against four aliens of Fleet Street for practising their craft without denization, in 1595 for a series of customs offences, and in 1596, a year of severe dearth, for market offences such as engrossing grain, buying cattle for resale, and buying cattle out of regular markets or fairs. But the mainstay of his informing activity in the nineties was the prosecution of brewers in or near the capital for exceeding the prices of beer and ale set by the

metropolitan authorities in accordance with the powers vested in them by a statute of 1532. Thus in 1592 he laid twenty-four such informations, in 1593 another twenty-two, in 1594 twenty-three, and a further thirty-one in 1598.[33]

The opportunities for intimidation and extortion that the business of informing offered made the 'promoters', as they were often called, a very unpopular group. A royal proclamation first issued in 1566, and reissued in 1594, complained that the courts at Westminster had been disturbed by 'light and evil disposed persons' beating up informers and making 'great outcries' against them.[34] At the heart of the complaints lay the fact that the informers were more interested in making a profit from breaches of the law than in its impartial enforcement. As Edward Coke put it, the informer 'doth vex and pauperise the subject and the community of the poorest sort, for malice or private ends and never for love of justice'.[35] Such a profession attracted men from shady and unreliable backgrounds, and encouraged them to act from the worst of motives. The court of Star Chamber in its censure of one Miles, a Suffolk informer in 1606, summed up a widely perceived stereotype: 'he was sometimes a Clothier in Suffolke, & not thryvinge in that trade, & envyinge the prosperitie and thryfte of other Clothyers there, he turned Common ynformer, & informed againste more then threescore of severall times, but never broughte any of them to any tryal, but merelye for vexatyon'.[36] Thus it was extremely rare for an information to be brought to a conclusion in the courts, the informer seeking to bring his victim to an out of court composition for the offence. This course was rendered attractive to defendants by the costs of litigation, and in particular by the irritating habit of the informers in bringing their actions in the courts at Westminster rather than at the quarter sessions or assizes in the county where the offence had been perpetrated. Compounding was supposedly subject to the control of the officers of the court where the information had been laid, but prior to legislation of 1576 which outlawed unlicensed compounding, the situation had been sufficiently vague for some informers to claim, as one did in an investigation of 1574, 'that he never made the courte privye nor dyd signyfye to the courte where his suyte did depende nor dyd not understande to the contrarye but that he mighte have compounded for his moytye at all tymes'.[37] Moreover, it is unclear how much difference the statute of 1576 made in practice. The decree and order books of the Exchequer record several licences to compound, subject to the proviso that the informer cause the defendant to bring in a penalty to the crown.[38] But such licences are hardly sufficient to account for the volume of unpursued informations. That abuses continued to flourish is demonstrated by the complaints brought against Edward Body, clothworker of London, judged worthy of censure by Star Chamber in 1596. He was accused of unlicensed compounding, using the threat that he had brought informations in the Exchequer to extort money when in fact no information had been laid, and compounding with offenders for an annual rent to discharge them from further proceedings in the Exchequer.[39]

The statutes of 1576 and 1589 are themselves testimony to the widespread sympathy felt within government circles for the popular outcry against informers. Reforming bills, which enjoyed Cecil's backing, failed in the Parliaments of 1566 and 1571, but the Council determined on action on its own account to discipline the informers.[40] In December 1574 the Lord Mayor instructed constables and churchwardens to appear before commissioners appointed to inquire into disorders committed by informers. This action coincided with Exchequer investigations into unlicensed compounding which resulted in the committal of several informers to the Fleet for infringements of orders taken by the Privy Council relating to Exchequer informing.[41] The clearest sign of official support for measures to curb abuses is the fact that the parliamentary measures of 1576 and 1589 were officially inspired: both bear the short-form enacting clause, and that of 1589 appears to have emerged from a committee of the law officers set up by the Council to look into law reform.[42]

However, for all the official sympathy for complaints against promoters, it has to be said that attitudes towards them were highly ambivalent. Parliament continued to pass statutes which were to be enforced by means of informer actions which could be brought by anyone.[43] Moreover, the existing literature perhaps underestimates the degree to which informers were found useful by those with an interest in law enforcement. City livery companies are frequently encountered making payments to informers for their services, particularly in the prosecution of practitioners of the trade who lacked the city freedom. In 1593 the Tallow Chandlers paid 40s. to William Calverley for his prosecution of alien candlemakers. Perhaps this was the unspecified 'cawse concerning the servyce of this Cytte' for which the City Chamberlain was instructed to pay Calverley and Gilbert Lillie 40s. in June 1592, for the aldermen are known to have been sympathetic to the complaints of the Tallow Chandlers against the strangers, fear of disorder against aliens being very strong in the city at this date.[44] Thus, although there is no conclusive evidence linking the Cutlers with Alley, his informations of 1594 against knifemakers may have been promoted at their behest, for this company shared in the anxiety about competition from the non-free in the later eighties and nineties, and is known to have paid some informers for their help.[45]

Even more intriguing is the possibility that Alley received some informal encouragement from the City, or even the Privy Council, in bringing his informations against brewers for exceeding the assize. Informations of this kind were not in fact usual, but show a strong tendency to cluster around periods of intense pressure from the city authorities on the drink trade. Each of the waves of informer activity against the brewers in 1564, 1573, and again in the years after 1592, when Alley was heavily involved, coincided with an unusual degree of civic hostility towards them.[46] In June 1592, for example, Common Council, noting the 'mislike had by the right honourable the Lordes and others of hir Maiesties most honorable privie Counsell as sundrie good citizens against the Brewers', set up committees to make recommendations to reform their abuses. In October the mayor announced revised prices and his intention to see them strictly enforced, while the Council instructed the Middlesex authorities to follow suit.[47] Official concern was renewed in the dearth conditions of 1596, and this time the Privy Council adopted a high profile in disciplining the brewers. In November the Council instructed the Lord Mayor to cause the brewers to enter bonds to observe the assize, and in succeeding months many leading brewers were required to appear before the Council for brewing at extreme rates. Meanwhile the aldermen instructed the wardmote inquests to make fortnightly certificates of brewers exceeding the prices. Moreover, the privy councillors now looked favourably on the suits depending in the Exchequer, deciding that in spite of strenuous lobbying by the brewers, the informations of Alley and others were to proceed.[48] Perhaps Burghley's successful petition for the city freedom for Alley in October 1597 is a sign that the informer's efforts were being gratefully acknowledged by the ageing Lord Treasurer and by the City. Another indication that Alley's activity against the brewers was welcome in the city is that in June 1599 the aldermen instructed their learned counsel to examine the informations brought by Alley and Brooke against the Southwark brewers, and the Bridgemasters to aid the informers with the books and charters in their possession.[49] It is unfortunate that no explicit connection between civic pressures and the informations can be made at an earlier stage, but the evidence suggests that at least the informers took their cue from city initiatives, and possibly that they also received some unofficial encouragement.

How far did Alley measure up to the contemporary stereotype of the promoter? He had, like Miles, the informer so roundly condemned by Star Chamber in 1606, exchanged one perfectly acceptable career for the hazards of informing. Moreover, suspicion would have focused on him because of his relatively low social status. Alley appears only fleetingly in the rate books of St Margaret Westminster, in 1587–90 and 1592–3, and then assessed at the lowest rate, 2*d.* per quarter. Poor rate was only paid by the top 50% of householders, so Alley came from the margins of that group.[50] He lacked that crucial passport to social acceptability, an assessment in the subsidy, for he does not appear on the extant assessment for St Margaret's of October 1600.[51] There is in fact considerable evidence that he suffered acute financial difficulties. Just as he was securing the freedom of the City in October 1597, he was outlawed for his failure to answer to a suit for a debt.[52] In May 1601, by which time Alley was in the City's employment, the Chamberlain was instructed to bail him out of the Counter from several actions, paying his creditors £12.[53] One might suppose that such impecuniosity might have tempted Alley into some of the more dubious rackets available to informers. However, there is no evidence against Alley in this respect, which is more than can be said for some of his fellow Exchequer informers in the nineties. The argument from silence is obviously vulnerable, but the confidence of the Lord Treasurer and the aldermen, no friends of wayward promoters, is not to be dismissed so lightly. Furthermore a close examination of Alley's informations can be used to present a more favourable picture of his activities than reference to the stereotypes might suggest.

It is true that the majority of Alley's informations apparently end with the enrolment of the information on the Memoranda Roll, and hence, one might assume, with a composition payment to Alley. Of the forty-six informations brought by Alley against brewers in 1592–3, twenty end at this point. In another twenty-three cases, the defendant appeared in court to plead not guilty and 'put himself on the country'. In only three cases did Alley take the proceedings further with efforts to empanel a jury. Although the deficiencies of the enrolment of proceedings on the Memoranda Rolls may mean that Alley was more diligent than the formal legal record suggests, it is likely that he compounded with many offenders.[54] In January 1594, for example, the ruling assistants of the Brewers' Company ordered that 'every man shoulde shifte for him sealfe and make his owne Attonement with the said promoters'.[55] But perhaps more significant is the fact that Alley did choose to pursue some of his informations *à l'outrance*, which for various reasons was a hazardous and highly frustrating undertaking.

It was hazardous and frustrating because it was slow and costly, because there were numerous devices available to defendants to pervert the course of justice, and because local juries were often unreliable. The appearance of the defendant was only the beginning of the battle, as the informer faced the uphill struggle of empanelling a jury. The Exchequer Barons would order the sheriff to empanel a jury to appear at Westminster to determine on the facts of the case, but almost invariably the sheriff would either fail to make a return, or the jury failed to appear, the case receiving successive adjournments in the meantime. The Barons would then dismiss the case to be tried at the local assizes by writ of *nisi prius*. Thus proceedings could be protracted. Alley waited two years before his information against Robert Marshall of Murcham for buying cattle out of fairs, came to trial at Nottinghamshire assizes at Easter 1598, and then the jury acquitted the defendant.[56]

Each stage of proceedings cost the informer money. The basic costs were not crippling, but in relation to the size of many recorded compositions, they must give us pause before concluding that Exchequer informing was a way to an easy profit. It cost 3*s.* 4*d.* to make an information, 3*s.* 4*d.* to enrol it, 2*s.* for every writ issued, 3*s.* 4*d.* for an attorney's fee each term the case continued, and 4s. for entering every continuance of term on the record.[57] The really crippling charges came if the case ran into disputes over legal technicalities and payments for counsel and motions in the court mounted up. In 1597 the Clothworkers' Company of London recovered the impressive forfeiture of £110 from Peter Collett, merchant of London, for the export of undressed cloth contrary to the provisions of a statute of 1566 passed for the company's benefit. But their expenditure on this suit was at least £86 17s. 1d. Unfortunately the accounts are not itemised, but consist of advances to the company's searchers who had brought the suit. The spiralling costs were doubtless due to the problems raised by Collett's contention that forty-two of the eighty cloths mentioned in the relevant information had in fact been the subject of an earlier information. The jury at Suffolk assizes brought a partial verdict, finding Collett guilty for two of the thirty-eight cloths, and referring the problem of the other forty-two to the Exchequer Barons, before whom the matter was argued in subsequent terms.[58] Costs of these dizzy heights were probably exceptional, but encounters with knotty legal problems were not. When Alley's information against the brewer Roger Bellowes came to trial at Guildhall the informer's counsel included Solicitor-General Egerton. In the event Bellowes escaped on a technicality, his counsel arguing that the information had been laid against the wrong person because it was the defendant's mother who had actually been running the business during the period covered by the information.[59] Alley's information against the brewer Abraham Campion ran into problems in the face of the latter's plea that the information was invalid because of Alley's recent outlawry.[60]

Exploiting legal technicalities was only one way by which Alley's opponents might hope to frustrate him. Some tried strong-arm tactics. In February 1593 the Barons heard that when Alley had tried to serve process on the servants of Abraham Campion to testify against their master, they had beaten him up.[61] If it did look as though people might testify against them, then the brewers might resort to intimidation. In 1598 Alley and Brooke complained to Star Chamber that Matthias Rutton of East Smithfield, the largest London brewer of his generation, had sought to frustrate the process of law by intimidating those whom the informers cited to give evidence against him. Alley and Brooke had served process on several victuallers who took their deliveries from Rutton. Those who were his tenants, the brewer threatened to turn out of doors if they testified against him; others he threatened with actions of debt or the stopping of credit. Others were encouraged to falsify their tallies, on which they recorded deliveries, to make it appear that they had received more barrels than was in fact the case, so that it would seem that the price paid per barrel was lower.[62]

Moreover, in attacking the brewers, Alley was taking on one of the best organised lobbies in London. Their lack of scruple emerges in the £100 bribe that they paid to Lord Keeper Puckering in April 1593 to defeat the aldermen's bill tightening the assize. On at least two occasions in the mid-nineties the company sought to lubricate the machinery of Exchequer process to stay the proceedings of the informers. In the autumn of 1593, and again in the summer of 1596, action on the informations against them was suspended as a result of the company's petitions concerning their recent losses accompanied by the generous greasing of the palms of Attorney-General Coke, and the Chancellor of the Exchequer's men.[63]

Alley did register some successes in the courts, but apparently not sufficient to solve his financial problems. The prospect of protracted litigation was sufficient to bring James Demetrius and Henry Cule, brewers, before the Barons to petition for a mitigated fine, a sign that Exchequer process tenaciously pursued held some terror. In spite of his efforts to browbeat potential witnesses, Matthias Rutton was found guilty on a partial verdict and sentenced to forfeit £36, of which £18 was to go to Alley and Brooke, the informers.[64] Alley's greatest success was secured against the Sussex ironmasters, for in this case a forfeiture of £495 was declared to be due to the informer, although it is not clear that the money was ever paid.[65] Alley's financial difficulties in the nineties make it hard to believe that he ever collected his portion.

Law enforcement for private profit did not inevitably mean a clash between the interests of the informer and the interests of the wider society. The offences that Alley informed against seem to have reflected the preoccupations of the Privy Council and the City. In his informations against the brewers Alley was striking at an unusually unpopular group within London; the informations against aliens reflected widespread anti-alien feeling; and the recently enacted statute of 1585 which formed the basis of his informations against the Sussex ironmasters was one for which the City had long been agitating.[66] It is true that a large number of Alley's informations remained unpursued, but the difficulties attendant upon Exchequer process mean that it is asking rather a lot to expect him to have pursued each and every one of them. It is significant that he appears to have made an effort to pursue one or two informations in most of the categories of offences he informed against. The really tantalising problem in assessing Alley's credentials as law enforcer is that of his compositions. We have no way of knowing either the size of the compositions he collected or their relationship to the costs of litigation in the Exchequer. Nor do we know whether his compositions had been licensed by the officers of the court. It should be emphasised that contemporaries found the principle of composition perfectly acceptable. Most would have baulked at the huge forfeitures claimed in the informations which if collected would have bankrupted defendants: hence the tendency for juries to bring partial verdicts finding the defendant liable for only a portion of the forfeiture claimed. Composition was readily accepted by those responsible for law enforcement within the city, and was not inevitably regarded as a passport to the continuing breach of the law. On the other hand it is fairly clear that the City kept a much tighter grip on the informers who used its courts: if Alley did play according to the rules, it is testimony to his good character and not to the diligence of the Exchequer.

HUGH ALLEY AND THE PROBLEMS OF THE MARKETS

The provisioning of the city at reasonable prices and the protection of the consumer were central to the responsibilities of the sixteenth-century metropolitan magistrate. The mayor's oath included the requirement that he look carefully to the assize of bread, ale, wine, fish, corn, flesh, and other victuals, and also weights and measures.[67] Thomas Norton, the City Remembrancer, in his advice to the mayor in 1574, underlined the magistrate's duties in this sphere: the mayor was to ensure that all victuals were of good and wholesome stuff, 'and by good foresight not to let slip the best times of providing or buying'.[68]

Some aspects of the mayor's discharge of these duties are well known. The City vigorously lobbied the Privy Council to bring pressure to bear upon country magistracies to release the grain the city needed. The aldermen organised the importation of Baltic grain in years of dearth, sold through the livery companies at prices slightly below those prevailing in the markets. Mark Benbow has demonstrated the energetic efforts of the city elite to enforce the assizes; taking bonds of victuallers to observe prices, using the wardmote inquests and patrols by civic officials to detect offenders, and deploying a wide range of sanctions against them. By city custom all fuel and victual brought to London by water could not be sold until a sample had been brought to the Lord Mayor and a price set by him upon the product. A large number of civic officers appointed by the mayor, the measurers of corn, salt, seacoals, and fruit, were responsible for overseeing sales and ensuring that the proper measures were observed.[69]

Much less well known, and largely because much harder to illuminate from the patchy source material, is the question of the nature of the regulation of the markets themselves. By the terms of the City's charter the office of clerk of the market was vested in the corporation.[70] Although there are signs that the Lord Mayor might become personally involved in the regulation of the markets in times of dearth when popular sensitivities demanded that the authorities be seen to be acting, the mayor's multifarious responsibilities ensured that in practice his functions in the markets devolved upon the officers of his household.[71]

Ubiquitous figures in civic government, most of the officers enjoyed specific responsibilities in the markets. Some appeared only fitfully: the principal serjeant carver conducting inspections of the bread sold in the city to see that the assize was being kept, the clerk and yeoman of the Chamber testing weights and measures, the serjeants of the Chamber gathering fines from the brewers for breaches of the assize and quality controls.[72] At the waterside the Waterbailiff occasionally disciplined fishwives, while the yeomen of the waterside ensured that no victuals brought to the city by water exceeded the mayor's price, and the yeomen of the woodwharves exercised similar functions with regard to the assize of wood.[73] Most important in the markets were the serjeant and yeoman of the channel, otherwise known as the serjeant and yeoman of the markets, the foreign taker, and the meal weighers. The three weighers of meal oversaw the meal markets to ensure that due measure was

Plate I

'*A Caveatt for the Citty of London*' *f.8*

Plate II

'A Caveatt for the Citty of London'   f.15

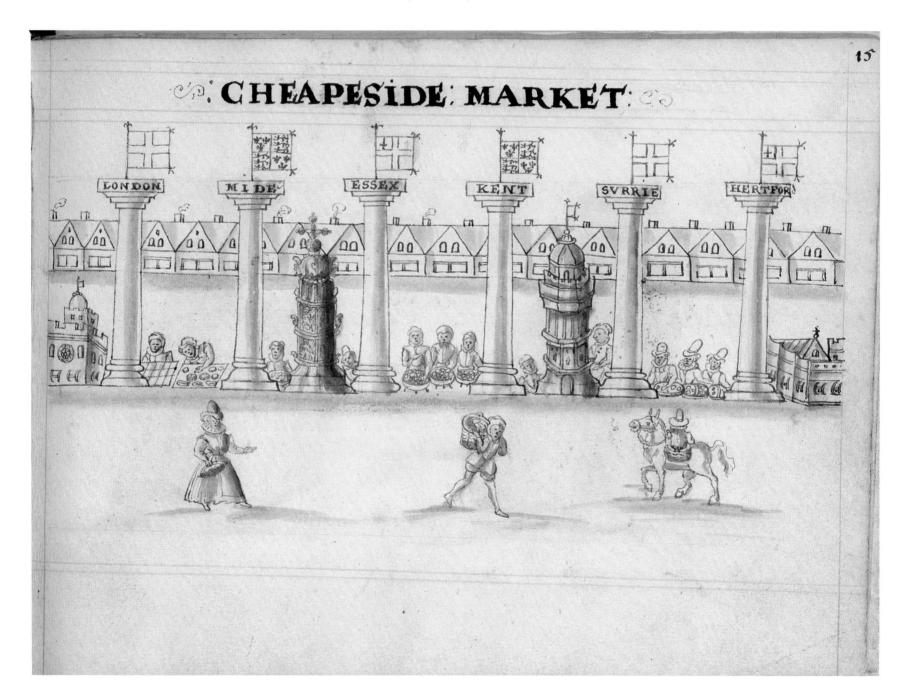

Plate III

'A Caveatt for the Citty of London'   f.19v

QVEENE HITHE WARDE

Plate IV

'A Caveatt for the Citty of London'   f.20

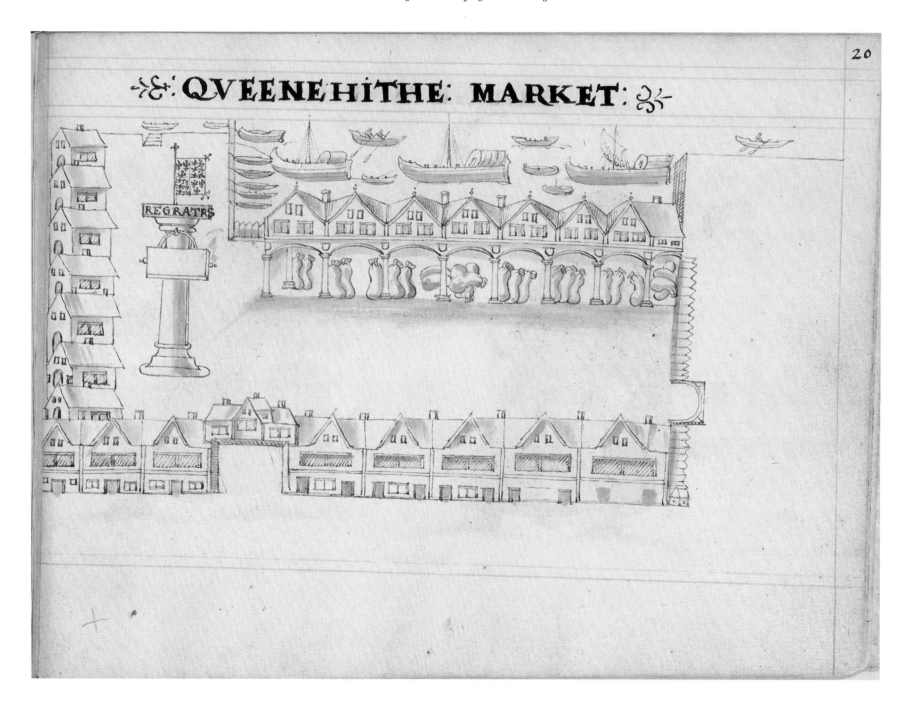

given and the mayor's price observed, that the meal put to sale was of the requisite quality, and that no meal was put to sale in inns or 'mispitched' as it was called.[74] The officers of the channel and the foreign taker had general responsibilities in seeing that the mayor's price was kept, which took them regularly into the markets to discipline a wide range of offenders.[75]

What kind of market offences did they prosecute? The most frequently appearing categories are sales outside the regular markets, particularly in inns, and regraters, forestallers and engrossers. Regrating, forestalling, and engrossing, the offences which also stood at the heart of Alley's reform scheme, were rather broadly defined. A statute of 1552 had defined forestallers as persons who intercepted goods en route to market or contracted to buy them before they were brought to market, regraters as persons who purchased goods in market with the intention of reselling them in the same market or another within a distance of four miles, and engrossers as persons who made purchases with the intention of reselling.[76] The rhetoric of the mid-century proclamations which sought to enforce the statute lashed out against 'the malice and naughty nature of a certain kind of people that live only for themselves'.[77] The attack on covetousness suggests that the intended victims were leading wholesalers playing the markets for easy profits. But the same offences were alleged against the petty traders, hucksters and fishwives who thronged the city streets, intercepting the produce they sold before it reached open market. In an overcrowded labour market this was one of the few areas of employment still open to women, but they were the victims of mounting hostility in the sixteenth century, blamed for increasing prices and viewed as sinks of lewdness, 'women', as a mayoral proclamation of 1590 put it, 'not onely of lewde and wicked life and behavior themselves but procurers and drawers of others also servauntes and such like to sundry wicked accions, the nomber of which people are of late yeres soe wonderfully encreased'.[78] The City authorities sought to limit the number of fishwives through a licensing system, operated initially through the aldermen in their wards, and from 1584 by the governors of Bridewell.[79] It was people of this kind who were most often apprehended by the officers of the mayor's household. Thus we find fines for 'certein heringe whiche were forstalled and ingroced by dyvers women', for 'halfe a pake of

small nuttes taken from a huxster for forstallinge and regratinge the same', for 'twoe baskettes cheryes engroced by an huxster', for 'a quarter of veele and certein Egges hawked'.[80]

However, by the fifteen-nineties it is clear that the officers of the household were retreating from involvement in the markets. The complaint of the act of Common Council of 1600 about the neglect of the officers formerly appointed to look to the markets is suppported by the evidence of the Book of Fines. The fines analysed by Mark Benbow show that in the period 1559–63, seventy-five fines were received for forestalling, regrating and engrossing, eighty-four for hawking, and fifty-eight for the sale of goods outside the market. The comparable figures for 1594–98 are twenty-nine, eight, and zero respectively.[81] Because of the difficulties attending law enforcement, the commitment of the officers was lukewarm. In the first place, the household officers ran the risk of counter-attacks being launched against them in the courts at Westminster. John Garfield recovered damages of 13*s*. 4*d*. from Ralph Shepard in King's Bench for the seizure of eggs which Shepard alleged had been forestalled.[82] Other problems occurred when defendants removed the suits against them from the City's jurisdiction to the courts at Westminster. Thus in 1598 the aldermen agreed that the Chamberlain should pay the costs of writs of *procedendo* for suits against brewers removed from the Mayor's Court to the higher courts.[83] The disincentives to efficient prosecution must have been considerably increased by the extra burdens on the officers of the household in the later years of Elizabeth's reign when, under the impact of war and dearth, their responsibilities proliferated.

The shortcomings of prosecution by the officers of the mayor's household led the aldermen to encourage the involvement of informers in economic regulation. Although it was open to any individual to bring informations in the Mayor's Court and several Exchequer informers availed themselves of the opportunity,[84] the aldermen also licensed individuals to inform, directing their attention at particular offences. Thus in 1573 Thomas Redknight, tallow chandler, was appointed to search for tallow which was intended to be sent out of the city or used in soap manufacture as well as for breaches of the assize of tallow. This activity involved him in the markets, for in 1575 he was instructed to survey the markets to determine whether the non-free butchers brought to the city all the tallow arising from their carcasses.[85] The City was perhaps more successful than the Exchequer in subjecting its informers to supervision from above. They were required to enter bonds barring them from compounding without the consent of the court and requiring them to pay costs in cases they failed to pursue.[86] Those informing on offences against the regulations relating to the Blackwell Hall cloth market, the city beams, and the garbelling of spices were supervised by the governors of St Bartholomew's and Christ's hospitals who insisted on examining offenders before legal action was commenced and determined the size of composition payments.[87]

Licensed informers were also used in the City's markets. In September 1589 Richard Martin, Lord Mayor, presented to the Court of Aldermen proposals for improving market regulation and disciplining hucksters, forestallers and regraters. The result was the appointment of eight citizens as informers and presenters of market offences. All offenders were to be certified to the mayor, and the City Chamber was to bear the costs of any litigation in which they became involved. For reasons which are unclear the scheme does not appear to have outlived Martin's mayoralty.[88] But it is clear that Alley's proposals for supplementing the established machinery of market regulation had their precursors. Moreover, Alley was not the only Exchequer informer upon whose services the city fathers drew. Like Alley, Rowland Wilkinson, minstrel, and William Dewsbury, clothworker, served as surveyors of beer while William Richbell was granted the office of Common Hunt in 1600.[89]

The initiative of 1589 represents one response to the growing concern about abuses in the markets, for which there is considerable evidence from the later fifteen-eighties. This can be documented most clearly through the presentments and petitions of the wardmote inquests. In addition to the presentment of infractions of civic regulations, these annually elected panels of middling householders in each ward, provided a platform for suggestions on areas of government on which action by the aldermen was necessary.[90] The petitions of the inquestmen of Cornhill ward were increasingly preoccupied with market abuses in the closing years of the sixteenth century. Almost every year from the late eighties they complained about forestalling, particularly by hucksters, fishwives, and sellers of oranges.[91] They were not afraid to criticise the failures of their rulers, accusing the clerk of the market in 1594 of failing to

comply with the requirement of the royal proclamation of 1587 for the regular trial of weights.[92] Effective rule depended on the responsiveness of the elite to criticisms of this kind.

Behind these demands for action from the aldermen lay several pressures. In the first place prices increased dramatically in the later eighties and nineties under the impact of successive harvest failures. Rappaport's composite price index averages 248 for the decade 1575–84, rising to 295 for 1585–94, an increase of 19%. Worse was to follow, as flour prices nearly tripled in the four years of harvest failure in the mid-nineties. For the decade 1595–1604, the composite index averaged 366, a further increase of 24% on the previous decade.[93] Price increases heightened sensitivity about infringements of market regulations, particularly where, as in the case of goods bought for resale, these infringements might be regarded as contributing to the increase in prices. Moreover, dearth heightened the social tensions which found expression in the hostility of the middling citizens to the disorderly poor, with whom the infringers of market regulations tended to be conflated. The nineties witnessed the elaboration of increasingly sophisticated machinery for the detection and punishment of hawkers, fishwives, colliers, second-hand dealers, rag-and-bone men, and more generally, the recent immigrants to the city from which the other groups were supposedly recruited.

The pressure from the wardmotes also reflected a perception that the existing machinery of market regulation was not working as efficiently as in the past. We have already seen how the officers of the mayor's household were retreating from involvement in the markets, probably under the pressure of widening responsibilities in other fields. More alarming still was the evidence which the nineties brought to light of corruption among the minor functionaries of civic administration. There was nothing new about complaints against the City's officials, as disputes over fees for their services were common, but the accusations of corruption and extortion which characterised the nineties were exceptional. In 1597 John Pate, foreign taker, an official with important responsibilities in the markets, was dismissed for taking money from colliers to conceal their offences in the use of sacks which did not keep proper measure.[94] The next year the aldermen appointed committees to investigate the abuses of the yeomen of the waterside 'who are soe careles and deale so badlie in the execucion of their office as that yt were much better for this Citty utterly to remove them'.[95] Throughout the later nineties the mayor was in dispute with the seacoalmeters. These struggles were partly matters of patronage, in particular the mayor's rights to appoint them and to a share of their profits, but they also reflected suspicions that the seacoalmeters were corrupt. In October 1596, for example, Thomas Maddoxe, dyer and seacoalmeter, was prosecuted for taking excessive fees and appointing deputies without bringing them to the Court of Aldermen to be sworn.[96]

The spectre of popular disorder in the event of the failure of the magistrates to meet popular expectations of good governance was a further stimulus to action in the markets. The extreme rarity of food riot in London made the disturbances of 1595 all the more alarming. On 12 and 13 June apprentices rioted over the price of fish and butter. In both sets of disturbances the apprentices appropriated some of the magisterial functions in the markets. A crowd of 300 apprentices assembled in Southwark on market day and took upon themselves the office of the clerk of the market, selling butter at 3*d.* per pound whereas the owners demanded 5*d.* They also issued a proclamation demanding that butter be brought to the market and not sold in inns or private houses.[97] The other disturbance occurred when apprentices, sent by their masters to purchase mackerel at Billingsgate, found that the stocks had been bought up by fishwives. A crowd of between sixty and eighty apprentices pursued the fishwives and took their fish, paying for it at the rate appointed by the Lord Mayor.[98] In attacking hucksters and those who sold in inns the apprentices were singling out groups and practices which were periodically the object of magisterial correction. However the appropriation of the duties of the magistrate in the markets is one sign that these duties were not being adequately discharged by the proper authorities. Sir John Spencer, the highly unpopular Lord Mayor, was heavily criticised in the wake of the disorders of 1595 for his failure to take appropriate action to remedy the dearth of victuals and for allowing civic officials to become negligent.[99]

The combination of high prices, with the evidence that the routine machinery of regulation was faltering, and with the threat of continuing popular disturbance if the authorities failed to act, explains the range of initiatives taken by the aldermen in the mid-nineties to tighten the regulation of the markets. Forestalling and regrating received renewed attention. In November 1594 Common Council passed an act providing for the disfranchisement of all found guilty of forestalling victuals and fuel, and in May 1595 appointed committees to look into measures that might be taken to curb regrating.[100] Meanwhile the aldermen disciplined a group of forestallers and regraters of corn at Billingsgate, and arranged for the indictment at the sessions of forestallers and regraters of fish.[101] The City's re-publication of its *Laws of the market* with its emphasis on measures against regrating and forestalling is another indication of official concern.[102] The problem of defective weights and measures was tackled in precepts to the wardmote inquests to search out unsealed weights, the preparation of indictments of those with unlawful weights and measures, and the public burning of unlawful measures in Cheapside.[103]

The experience of the mid-nineties was such that the reformist momentum was sustained in the years of lower prices which followed. William Jaggard's pamphlet *A view of all the right honourable the lord mayors of London* suggests that the three mayors at the turn of the century, under whose rule Alley's scheme came to fruition, all enjoyed reputations as righters of wrongs in the markets. Soame, Moseley and Rider were complimented for their efforts to reform defective weights, to enforce the assize of bread, and to deal with market abuses in general.[104] The evidence of the Repertories confirms these plaudits. Particularly impressive is the sustained drive to reform weights and measures. New measures were ordered for seacoals, corn and salt, and scales provided in all the markets. Arrangements were made for the seizure of defective weights by two members of the Founders' Company, and for their recasting by the keeper of the Guildhall according to the Exchequer standard[105]. City concern over the variety of measures in use at this date probably explains the revival of interest in the Exchequer in the standardisation of weights and measures throughout England. The proclamation of 1587 had re-established standard weights; in 1600 the Exchequer began trials of measures, the results of which formed the basis of attempted remedy through legislation in Parliament in 1601 and by royal proclamation early the following year when the bills failed.[106]

CONCLUSION

Alley's scheme therefore fits into a range of initiatives apparently energetically pursued by the aldermen in response to the deteriorating economic conditions of the fifteen-nineties and pressure from the wardmotes. It is, however, difficult to assess the impact of this activity. The evidence does not allow us to determine how readily the wards responded to orders for action from the aldermen, nor can we tell how typical are the instances of the disciplining of individual offenders in the absence of full judicial records. The juxtaposition of draconian legislation against forestallers from Common Council in the autumn of 1594 with the popular indictment of the failures of the magistrates in the riots of the following summer suggests the need to differentiate between magisterial rhetoric and practice. It is true that the aldermen did enough to maintain the fragile fabric of order in the capital in subsequent years. The publicity given to the punishment of heinous offenders was one way in which a little effort by the rulers could be made to go a long way. But there are some indications that the initiatives of the nineties had serious limitations. By this date the assize was enforced on a much narrower range of commodities than had been the case in the sixties and seventies: bread and beer remained at the heart of the aldermen's concerns, but wood, tallow, and wine had been abandoned. Moreover, the aldermen were increasingly reluctant to use some of the standard devices of the sixties and seventies in enforcing the assizes, such as recognisances by victuallers to observe specified prices, and the use of regular searches by the wardmote inquests to detect offenders.[107] Even more intriguing is the possibility that whereas earlier the aldermen had been willing to discipline wholesalers for profiteering, by the nineties the main thrust of their activity was against petty traders, fishwives and hucksters. Wholesalers, like the London dealers in butter and cheese prosecuted in the Exchequer in 1595, were left to the attention of the professional Exchequer informers.[108] Once again the absence of court records for the city makes it difficult to substantiate this argument conclusively, but there are more instances of wholesalers being proceeded against by the aldermen in the mid-Tudor decades than in the nineties, and they were much more frequently an object of legislation by Common Council in the earlier period: against the rather

unimpressive legislative achievement of the nineties should be set enactments of 1571 and 1574 against citizens riding into the country to buy up butter, cheese, and wood, and the action taken by the aldermen in 1576 against brewers profiteering from the resale of the grain they had purportedly purchased for use in brewing, and regular action against the engrossers of tallow and wood.[109] The increasing preoccupation with the petty dealers reflects mounting hostility to the misdemeanours of the poorer sort in the more socially polarised conditions of the nineties.

Finally, Alley's career allows us an opportunity to reflect on the character of law enforcement at the national and local level. The practice of allowing successful informers a portion of the fines was widely accepted, encouraged by the Corporation and the Privy Council. The line between officially sponsored 'bureaucratic' enforcement, and enforcement by private individuals for their own benefit, was blurred because civic officials with responsibilities in law enforcement, like the officers of the mayor's household, were expected to supplement their meagre salaries not only with fees for their services but also with portions of the fines on the offences they detected, and because informers might be subject to the control of the aldermen or Chamberlain or at least might receive some official encouragement. Enforcement by informer action did not necessarily mean that the enforcement of the law was hopelessly compromised by the motive of private profit. But it seems that the City was more successful than the Exchequer in checking the abuses that informer-sponsored enforcement offered. This was because, in the first place, the aldermen enjoyed the services of a larger bureaucracy. The concentration of economic activity in the city together with the opportunities it offered to raise revenue through tolls bred a large number of officials whose functions included the presentment of breaches of city regulations.[110] Although the officials displayed some markedly non-bureaucratic characteristics, not least because they usually held their offices for life, the Corporation nevertheless retained some sanction over their activities as the aldermen's frequent interventions to discipline their misdemeanours testify. Secondly, where private informers did become involved in law enforcement, the aldermen took pains to regulate them. This is suggested by the recognisances taken from the informers to the Chamber for their just dealing, by the regular interventions of the Court of Aldermen in proceedings in the Mayor's Court, and by the close control exercised by the governors of the hospitals of St Bartholomew's and Christ's over informations for breaches of the regulations concerning the payment of hallage on cloth sales, the garbelling of spices, and the weighing of goods at the city beams. Alley's scheme illustrates both the willingness of the Corporation to allow private profit in securing the enforcement of the laws and the degree of control the aldermen were prepared to exercise in order to prevent the abuses to which informing so readily gave rise.

NOTES

[1] K. Muir (ed.), *Thomas Middleton, Three Plays* (1975), p. 22 ('A Chaste Maid in Cheapside', II. ii. 53–6).

[2] CLRO, Rep. 24, f. 137.

[3] Ibid., ff. 351v, 435.

[4] Ibid., f. 459.

[5] CLRO, Journal 25, ff. 150v–152.

[6] Ibid. For forestalling, regrating and engrossing see above, pp. 5–6.

[7] Stow, i, pp. lxiii–lxv. Alley served as surveyor of beer in 1601: CLRO, Journal 25, f. 283v.

[8] CLRO, Book of Fines, f. 233.

[9] See below, pp. 23–4.

[10] CLRO, Rep. 25, ff. 187, 246v.

[11] Ibid., ff. 236v, 237.

[12] GL, MS 5570/1, p. 289.

[13] CLRO, Journal 25, f. 332.

[14] See below, p. 23

[15] See below, p. 22.

[16] A. M. Burke (ed.), *Memorials of St Margaret's Church Westminster: the Parish Registers, 1539–1660* (1914), pp. 16, 227.

[17] WPL, Will Register, Bracy, f. 73.

[18] Westminster Abbey Muniments, Lease Book v, f. 131v; ix, f. 88.

[19] WPL, E5, accts. for 1578–80 and 1580–2.

[20] WPL, E146–7.

[21] WPL, E2413, f. 3; E6.

[22] GL, MS 9222/1 (burial of Hugh Alley, 4 December 1602); 9050/4, f. 274v (administration of goods of Hugh Alley of St Botolph Aldgate granted to son Edward Alley, 1604).

[23] Westminster Abbey Muniments, 36924; Lease Book vii, f. 163; WPL, Will Register Elsam, f. 545.

[24] PRO, E351/3210–16. See also Julia Merritt's forthcoming thesis, 'Local Government and social change in Westminster parishes, 1500–1625'.

[25] WPL, E5, acct. for 1596–8, f. 22.

[26] GL, MS 6122/1, accts. for 1597–8.

[27] WPL, E5, acct. for 1588–9, f. 12v.

[28] P. L. Hughes and J. F. Larkin (eds.), *Tudor Royal Proclamations* (3 vols, 1964, 1969), II, 543–8; F. A. Youngs, *The Proclamations of the Tudor Queens* (1976), pp. 37–8.

[29] WPL, E2413, f. 3.

[30] CLRO, Rep. 25, f. 237v.

[31] On informers see M. G. Davies, *The Enforcement of English Apprenticeship, 1563–1642* (Cambridge, Massachusetts, 1956); G. R. Elton, 'Informing for Profit: a Sidelight on Tudor Methods of Law Enforcement', *Cambridge Historical Journal*, 11 (1954), pp. 149–67; M. W. Beresford, 'The Common Informer, the Penal Statutes and Economic Regulation', *Economic History Review*, second series, 10 (1957–8), pp. 221–37; D. R. Lidington, 'Mesne Process in Penal Actions at the Elizabethan Exchequer', *The Journal of Legal History*, 5 (1984), pp. 33–8.

[32] PRO, E159/399, Mich. 32 Eliz., recorda, rots. 201–5, 223, 295.

[33] PRO, E159/407, Mich. 36 Eliz., recorda, rots. 237–8 (aliens); E159/410, Hil. 38 Eliz., recorda, rots. 50, 113, Eas. 38 Eliz., recorda, rots. 65, 76; E159/411, Mich. 38 Eliz., recorda, rot. 243 (marketing offences); E159/408, Hil. 37 Eliz., recorda, rot. 189, Eas. 37 Eliz., recorda, rot. 25; E159/409, Trin. 37 Eliz., recorda, rot. 20 (customs offences); E159/402, Eas. 34 Eliz., recorda, rots. 270–298; E159/404, Hil. 35 Eliz., recorda, rots. 240–55, 270–6, 350–3, 355, Eas. 35 Eliz., recorda, rot. 51; E159/406, Hil. 31 Eliz., recorda, rots. 115–31; E159/414, Hil. 40 Eliz., recorda, rots. 90–2, Eas. 40 Eliz., recorda, rots. 116, 119, 135–46, 173; E159/415, Mich. 40 Eliz., recorda, rots. 218–26, 231 (brewers).

[34] *Tudor Royal Proclamations*, II, pp. 288–9; III, p. 143.

[35] Beresford, 'Common Informer', p. 221.

[36] W. P. Baildon (ed.), *Les Reportes del Cases in Camera Stellata, 1593 to 1609* (1894), pp. 300–1. The outline of informers' abuses is based on the various proposals for reform: PRO, SP15/20/22, ff. 46–49; E175/6/25–27; BL, Harleian MS 249/17, ff. 114–118; *Statutes of the Realm*, IV, 18 Eliz, c. 5; 31 Eliz. c. 5. See also Davies, *Enforcement*, chs. ii–iii.

[37] PRO, E133/2/241, examination of William Ebbes of Newington.

[38] Examples: PRO, E123/19, ff. 5, 10, 17, 37v, 110v, 227.

[39] Baildon (ed.), *Reportes*, p. 63; PRO, STAC5/S37/28. For complaints of continued unlicensed compounding see Davies, *Enforcement*, p. 74; PRO, E112/27/240; W. le Hardy (ed.), *Middlesex Sessions Records*, new series, I, pp. 246–7.

[40] A. Hassell-Smith, *County and Court: Government and Politics in Norfolk, 1558–1603* (1974), pp. 116–20; *Calendar of State Papers Domestic, Addenda, 1566–79*, pp. 20–2; PRO, SP 15/20/22, ff. 46–9.

[41] CLRO, Journal 20, f. 189 (I have not traced any record of the issue of the commission, nor of the orders of the privy council referred to in the disciplining of the informers); PRO, E123/6, ff. 69, 74, 80, 100v; E133/2/241, 242, 255, 279, 284: examinations in February–May 1575.

[42] *Statutes of the Realm*, IV, 18 Eliz. I c. 5, 31 Eliz. I c. 5. On enacting clauses see G. R. Elton, 'Enacting Clauses and Legislative Initiative, 1559–71', *Bulletin of the Institute of Historical Research*, 53 (1980), pp. 183–91; D. M. Dean, 'Enacting Clauses and Legislative Initiative, 1584–1601', *Bulletin of the Institute of Historical Research*, 57 (1984), pp. 140–8, esp. pp. 141, n. 8, 142.

[43] Beresford, 'Common Informer', p. 222, notes that of the 115 penal statutes still in force in James' reign, thirty originated in the reign of Elizabeth.

[44] GL, MS 6152/2, f. 31; CLRO, Rep. 22, f. 387; Journal 23, ff. 111v–112. For other instances of company sponsored informer action see Goldsmiths' Company, Reg. K, pp. 213, 272, 277; Merchant Tailors Company, C. M. iii, ff. 367, 401v, 437; GL, MSS 14346/1, f. 195v; 7151/1, ff. 38, 39, 59v.

[45] CLRO, Rep. 21, f. 280; GL, MS 7147/1, pp. 24, 25, 40, 116, 117.

[46] PRO, E159/348, Trin. 6 Eliz., recorda, rots. 93–135, Mich. 6 Eliz., recorda, rots. 130–181, 521–525; E159/365, Mich. 15 Eliz., recorda, rots. 370–400.

[47] CLRO, Journal 23, f. 111v; Rep. 22, f. 438r–v; *A.P.C.*, xxiii, 277; BL, Cotton MS Titus F ii, ff. 84, 88v, 91v; GL, MS 5442/5, acct. for 1592–3.

[48] *APC.* xxvi, pp. 327, 499, 506–7, 535, 536, 539, 540; xxvii, pp. 97–8; CLRO, Journal 24, ff. 191v, 207.

[49] CLRO, Rep. 24, f. 419v.

[50] WPL, E146–7.

[51] PRO, E179/142/235. Other informers did rather better: William Brooke assessed at £5 in the same year (ibid.); Clement Bankes assessed at £5 in 1599 (PRO, E179/146/382), and William Dewsbury assessed at £3 in 1582 (PRO, E179/251/16, m. 79).

[52] PRO, STAC5/52/30, demurrer of Lambert Smith; E159/414, Eas. 40 Eliz., recorda, rot. 143.

[53] CLRO, Rep. 25, ff. 236v, 242.

[54] Lidington, 'Mesne Process', pp. 34–6.

[55] GL, MS 5445/9, 10 Jan. 1594.

[56] PRO, E159/410, Eas. 38 Eliz., recorda, rots. 76, 11.

[57] Davies, *Enforcement*, p. 278.

[58] PRO, E 159/409, Trin. 37 Eliz., recorda, rot. 23; Clothworkers' Company, Quarter Wardens' Accounts (QWA), 1595–6, f. 5v; QWA, 1596–7, ff. 6v, 12v–13; Renter Wardens' Accounts, 1596–7, f. 8v; QWA, 1597–8, f. 10v. It was the company's usual practice to compound with offenders after informing against them in the Exchequer.

[59] GL, MS 5445/9, 25 May 1593.

[60] PRO, E159/414, Eas. 40 Eliz., recorda, rot. 143.

[61] PRO, E123/20, f. 52.

[62] PRO, STAC5/A52/30; E159/414, Hil. 40 Eliz., recorda, rot. 92.

[63] GL, MSS 5445/9, Oct. 1593, 7 June 1596; 5442/5, acct. for 1596–7.

[64] PRO, E159/414, Hil. 40 Eliz., recorda, rots. 91, 92.

[65] PRO, E159/399, Mich. 32 Eliz., recorda, rots. 201–205; E159/400, Hil. 33 Eliz., recorda, rot. 139; E123/17, f. 269; E123/20, f. 85. The last we hear of the case is the petition of Richard Michelborne, one of the defendants that process of execution for the queen's moiety be awarded against his co-defendants.

[66] G. R. Elton, *The Parliament of England, 1559–1581* (1986), pp. 244–5; CLRO, Rep. 17, f. 311v.

[67] BL, Additional MS 2177, f. 2.

[68] J. P. Collier (ed.), *Illustrations of Old English Literature* (3 vols, 1866), III, item 8, p. 12.

[69] N. S. B. Gras, *The Evolution of the English Corn Market from the Twelfth to the Eighteenth Century* (Harvard Economic Studies, XIII, 1915); M. Benbow, 'The Court of Aldermen and the Assizes: the Policy of Price Control in Elizabethan London', *Guildhall Studies in London History*, 4 (1981), pp. 93–118; P. V. McGrath, 'The Marketing of Food, Fodder and Livestock in the London Area in the Seventeenth Century with Special Reference to the Sources of Supply' (London M.A. dissertation, 1948).

[70] G. Norton, *Commentaries on the History, Constitution and Chartered Franchises of the City of London* (1869), pp. 346, 355, 374–5, 387.

[71] CLRO, Rep. 14, f. 320; Rep. 24, f. 102; B. R. Masters, 'The Mayor's Household before 1600', in A. E. J. Hollaender and W. Kellaway (eds), *Studies in London History presented to P. E. Jones* (1969), pp. 95–114.

[72] Masters (ed.), *Chamber Accounts*, pp. 4, 15, 64, 69; GL, MSS 5174/1–2; CLRO, Chamber Accounts, sixteenth century series, i, ff. 21, 116.

[73] Masters (ed.), *Chamber Accounts*, pp. 31, 83; CLRO, Book of Oaths, ff. 13v–14v, 25v–26; Rep. 18, f. 59v; Rep. 21, ff. 113, 218v, 328, 428, Rep. 21, ff. 80v, 116; Rep. 24, ff. 179v, 199v; Rep. 27, f. 10; PRO, STAC5/E16/6, E2/23, E5/31.

[74] CLRO, Book of Oaths, ff. 45–6; Rep. 17, f. 434v; Rep. 23, f. 91.

[75] CLRO, Book of Oaths, ff. 21v–22v, 36v–37.

[76] *Statutes of the Realm*, IV, 5 & 6 Edw. VI. c. 14.

[77] *Tudor Royal Proclamations*, I, pp. 520–1, 526–7.

[78] CLRO, Journal 22, f. 378v; Journal 24, f. 98v.

[79] CLRO, Journal 17, ff. 299v–300; Rep. 17, f. 86; Rep. 21, f. 115.

[80] CLRO, Book of Fines, passim.

[81] CLRO, Misc. MSS 363.3, analysis of fines by Mark Benbow.

[82] Masters (ed.), *Chamber Accounts*, pp. 35, 92. For other examples see CLRO, Rep. 20, f. 392 (suits against Waterbailiff for taking unlawful fish in Cheapside, and for seizure of cheeses as foreign bought and sold); Rep. 20, ff. 70, 74 (Thomas Redknight prisoner in the Gatehouse Westminster in execution of £12); Rep. 19, f. 466 (suit in King's Bench against Manning and Byrom, yeomen of the woodwharves); Rep. 22, f. 126v (suit against Philip Treharne for taking cloths by appointment of Sir George Bond when Lord Mayor); PRO, C24/136, Clark vs. Manning and Byrom (dispute over attachment of faggots by the yeomen of the woodwharves for not being according to the assize).

[83] CLRO, Rep. 24, ff. 221v, 272.

[84] Notably Rowland Wilkinson, minstrel and Edward Jennings, fishmonger: CLRO, MC1/12/49; MC1/219/130; MC1/12/17–18, 20, 48.

[85] Redknight lacked a formal position in the household until 1583 when he was appointed yeoman of the woodwharves, but he was described as an officer to the Chamber before then: CLRO, Rep. 18, ff. 78, 97v, 100v, 101r–v, 337, 384; Rep. 20, f. 451v; GL, MS 12806/2, f. 322v. For other informers to the Chamber see St Bartholomew's Hospital (SBH), Hal/2, ff. 203, 204, 205v, 219v, 231v, 236; Hal/3, f. 7; CLRO, MC1/5B/184, 8/125, 9/24 (Thomas Johnson); SBH, Hal/2, ff. 235v, 273; Hal/3, f. 61v; CLRO, MC1/10/43; above, n. 59 (Gilbert Lillie).

[86] CLRO, Rep. 18, f. 337; Rep. 19, f. 180v.

[87] SBH, Hal/2, f. 165.

[88] CLRO, Rep. 22, ff. 91, 93v–94, 97v, 107.

[89] CLRO, Rep. 22, f. 382v; Journal 24, ff. 219, 310; Journal 25, f. 69 (Wilkinson); Journal 24, f. 310; Journal 25, f. 69 (Dewsbury); Rep. 25, ff. 170–172 (Richbell).

[90] V. Pearl, 'Change and Stability in Seventeenth-Century London', *London Journal*, 5 (1979), 20, 25.

[91] GL, MS 4069/1, ff. 44, 49, 51, 54, 56, 60, 62v, 65, 67, 71v, 83, 87.

[92] Ibid., f. 62v.

[93] I am grateful to Professor Rappaport for generously making available some of the raw data on which his conclusions are based. Cf. S. Rappaport, 'Social Structure and Mobility in Sixteenth-Century London: Part I', *London Journal*, 9 (1983), 128–9.

[94] CLRO, Rep. 24, ff. 70r–v, 127v–128. Cf. Rep. 23, f. 444v; Rep. 24, ff. 63, 64, 67v.

[95] CLRO, Rep. 24, f. 208v.

[96] CLRO, MC1/219/131; Rep. 23, f. 585. Cf. Journal 23, f. 329v; Journal 24, f. 126v; Rep. 23, f. 561.

[97] BL, Harleian MS 2143, f. 57v; J. Stow, *The Annales or Generall Chronicle of England* (1615), p. 769.

[98] CLRO, Remembrancia ii, no. 97.

[99] *Historical Manuscripts Commission, Hatfield*, V, 248–50.

[100] CLRO, Journal 23, f. 334; Journal 24, f. 3.

[101] CLRO, Rep. 23, ff. 391, 405v–406.

[102] *The Laws of the Market* (1595).

[103] CLRO, Rep. 22, ff. 382, 415, 465v, 519v, 547.

[104] W. Jaggard, *A View of all the Right Honourable the Lord Mayors of London* (1601).

[105] CLRO, Rep. 24, ff. 314v, 465v–466, 479; Rep. 25, ff. 27v, 38v–39, 44v, 55–56, 65r–v.

[106] The Exchequer trials are outlined in the proclamation of 1602: *Tudor Royal Proclamations*, III, pp. 241–5. In May 1600 the Keeper of the Guildhall was instructed to carry the city's bushel, gallon and pint to Vincent Skinner for trial at the Exchequer: CLRO, Rep. 25, f. 91v. For the three bills of 1601 see PRO, SP12/282/48, ff. 98–99; SP12/283/3, ff. 3–4; SP12/283/7, ff. 10–15.

[107] Benbow, 'Assizes'.

[108] PRO, E159/409, Mich. 37 Eliz., recorda, rots. 383–400, 437.

[109] CLRO, Journal 19, ff. 325v, 326, 330–331v; Journal 20, ff. 131v–132v; Rep. 19, ff. 129v, 130v, 170v–171, 366; Rep. 20, ff. 34, 109v.

[110] F. F. Foster, *The Politics of Stability. A Portrait of the Rulers of Elizabethan London* (1977), pp. 173–9.

THE HISTORY OF THE MANUSCRIPT

Hugh Alley's *Caveat* now belongs to the Folger Shakespeare Library in Washington, DC. It was acquired in 1928 from the London booksellers Maggs Brothers Ltd, who had bought it at a sale earlier that year of the papers of Major Hugh Edward Wilbraham of Delamere House, Northwich, Cheshire.[1]

It seems possible that the manuscript had been in the possession of the Wilbraham family almost since its compilation, though it was not mentioned in the Historical Manuscripts Commission Reports on the family's MSS in 1872 and 1874.[2] A note on one of the otherwise blank pages of the book (f. 24; see Figure 2) reads 'Richd Wilbraham Esqr married Elizabeth Daughter of Sr Thos Pollicill Kt Ld Mayor of London Anno Domini: 1585', in a seventeenth- or possibly early eighteenth-century hand. This couple were the direct ancestors of Major H. E. Wilbraham, though it is not of course certain that they possessed the MS.[3]

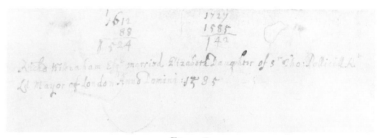

Figure 2

Richard Wilbraham, who died in 1601, was the City's Common Serjeant, a legal office of high status. Although he was only elected to the office earlier that year he had been deputy to the previous Common Serjeant since 1585, and apparently exercised the office in full since at least 1588. He is sometimes referred to as Common Serjeant (not merely deputy) in the period before 1601. He only became a freeman in 1586, when he bought or was given the freedom of the Drapers' Company, to which Pollicill, by then his father-in-law, also belonged. Clearly, if Wilbraham acquired Alley's manuscript, he must have done so very shortly after it was written. His descendants appear to have been based at Nantwich in Cheshire, whence he himself came, and the family took no further part in City affairs.[4]

It seems less likely that the MS was acquired by Wilbraham's father-in-law Sir Thomas Pollicill, though he survived the former by some years. Pollicill, more usually spelt Pullison or Pullyson, was bound apprentice to a Draper in

1541, and probably therefore became a freeman in 1548 or 1549. He was elected Alderman in 1573 and Lord Mayor in 1584–5, but retired from the Court of Aldermen in 1588, on plea of infirmity. According to Beaven, he lived to a great age (he was still alive in 1616), but 'fell on evil days', and was granted a pension by the Court of Aldermen. By 1598, therefore, he was no longer a person of importance in the city.[5]

On the same page (f. 24), and in the same hand, as the memorandum about the Wilbraham-Pollicill marriage, there are also some figures or calculations:

1612	1727
88	1585
1524	142

but the purport of these is not clear. Possibly the first set are calculations about Sir Thomas Pollicill's age; he could well have been born in 1524, and would therefore have been 88 in 1612, though why that should be significant is obscure. The second sum could be calculating the years elapsed since the marriage referred to, though the hand in which all the memoranda are written does not appear to be as late as 1727.

It is hard to see why either Wilbraham or Pollicill should have been in possession of the manuscript. It was clearly presented to the Lord Mayor, Saltonstall, to whom it was dedicated. Alley's proposals assigned no particular role to the Common Serjeant in the prosecution of market offences in his scheme. The coincidence of name and descent, however, seems strongly to suggest that it did pass directly to the Wilbraham family; it is conceivable that it happened to be temporarily in Wilbraham's hands for some reason at the time of his rather early death, and remained with his personal papers thereafter. The limited success of Alley's proposals might explain why the City did not subsequently seek to recover the manuscript.[6]

Wherever it was held, the manuscript does not seem to have been at all well-known until the twentieth century, when it appears to have been exhibited in London prior to sale. Several authors have since used one or two of the topographical scenes as illustrations, but the *Caveat* has not been reproduced in its entirety, or on this scale, until now.[7]

It was not entirely lost to sight in the intervening centuries, however: drawn copies of two of the scenes (Billingsgate and

Eastcheap) are included in the 'Crowle Pennant', an extra-illustrated copy of Thomas Pennant's *Some Account of London* (3rd edition, 1793). As was fairly common at the time, the original volumes of Pennant's work have been disbound and used to form the core of a scrapbook of drawings and engravings of maps, portraits, and topographical views illustrating London's history. The 'Crowle Pennant', in the British Museum, Department of Prints and Drawings, bears the bookplate of Charles Crowle, Esq., but elsewhere is ascribed to William Crowle, for whom the engraver John Thomas Smith produced drawings and plates. The drawings from Alley's manuscript occur in volume x (not foliated), in the appropriate position to illustrate Pennant's text.[8]

Most of the illustrations added to the 'Crowle Pennant' are prints and engravings, but the Alley copies are drawings in pen and wash. That the artist saw the manuscript itself is suggested by the caption to the Billingsgate drawing: 'Drawn in a MS by Hugh Alley, citizen and plumber [*sic*] 1598, in which he inveighs against Engrossers and regrators, but without any argument to support his opinion'. The caption to Eastcheap merely says 'From a very old drawing. Vide Dr Combe'.[9] It is perhaps surprising that only two of the thirteen market scenes were copied, and also that, once copied and presumably shown to other collectors at the time, they were not more widely reproduced thereafter.[10]

NOTES

[1] Folger Shakespeare Library, Washington, DC, USA, MS V.a.318, ff. 145.2; S. de Ricci with W. J. Wilson, *Census of Medieval and Renaissance Manuscripts in the United States and Canada* (New York, 1935–40), no. 1824.1.

[2] Royal Commission on Historical Manuscripts, *Third Report* (1872), Appendix, pp. 292–3; idem, *Fourth Report* (1874), Appendix, pp. 416–17.

[3] Burke, *Landed Gentry* (18th edn, 1965), I, under Wilbraham.

[4] B. R. Masters, 'City Officers I: the Common Serjeant', *Guildhall Miscellany*, 2 (9), (1969), 379–89; A. H. Johnson, *The History of the Worshipful Company of the Drapers of London*, II (1915), 148, 194; P. Boyd, *Roll of the Drapers' Company of London* (1934), under Wilbraham; F. F. Foster, *The Politics of Stability, a Portrait of the Rulers of Elizabethan London* (1977), p. 188.

[5] A. B. Beaven, *The Aldermen of the City of London*, I (1908), 157, 208; II (1913), 39, 173; Boyd, *Roll of the Drapers*, under Pullison; Foster, *Politics*, p. 164.

[6] See above, p. 15–16, for the history of Alley's proposals.

[7] De Ricci's *Census* (see n. 1) refers to a London exhibition, probably the Maggs' sale. One or two of the drawings are reproduced in Thomas Burke, *The streets of London through the centuries* (1940), pls 8 and 9; J. Hurstfield (ed.),

Tudor Times (Historical Association pamphlet, 1964), pl. 9; Levi Fox, *Shakespeare's England* (1972), p. 86; A. R. H. Baker and J. B. Harley (ed.), *Man made the land* (1973), fig. 159, p. 124; P. E. Jones, *The Butchers of London* (1976), pls 12, 13; H. Hobhouse, *The Ward of Cheap in the City of London, a short history* (n.d., post-1958), pl. 2, f. p. 49; and probably elsewhere. I am grateful to Joy Thwaytes for drawing my attention to the Historical Association pamphlet, which curiously refers to the drawings as woodcuts.

[8] British Museum, Department of Prints and Drawings; Bernard Adams, *London Illustrated, 1604–1851* (1983), p. xviii.

[9] The reference to 'Dr Combe' has been pursued without success so far. It could refer to the author William Combe (1741–1823), 'Doctor Syntax' (see Adams, *London Illustrated*, index); or possibly the Charles Combe, MD, whose 'valuable and extensive collection of prints' was sold at auction in 1803 (Sale catalogue, British Library (Printed Books), 821.g.18 (7)). In either case it suggests that someone else knew about the original.

[10] The Crowle Pennant copies of Alley's drawings are reproduced, possibly for the first time, in F. Barker and P. Jackson, *London, 2000 years of a city and its people* (1974), p. 91. It is hoped that the reproduction of the whole of the 'Caveat' here may evoke reports of further 'sightings' of the drawings.

THE VALUE OF
HUGH ALLEY'S 'CAVEAT'

At first glance Hugh Alley's *Caveat* might seem to be merely quaint and amusing, a possible source for one or two useful topographical details but, otherwise, a booklet whose main value might seem to lie rather in the scarcity of pictures of London in the late sixteenth century than in any intrinsic merits of its own. But the editors have found that the more they have studied Alley's drawings, the more impressed they have become with his work, and indebted to him for the insights which he provides into the market life of London in the 1590s. Hugh Alley was not an artist like Van Wyngaerde, nor a surveyor like Ralph Treswell, nor a self-taught man of learning like John Stow, but he was energetic, genuinely concerned to eradicate malpractices in the food markets of London and he had a vision which, while being rooted in the streets and stalls, people and shops of his native city, suffused London in a cloud of righteousness and justice.[1] The influence of religious writing and preaching is redolent in every line of Alley's prefatory remarks. But whereas the energies of many reformers are taken up in speech, Hugh Alley went further and put pen to paper

and compiled a document which was sufficiently striking in its own time to have been preserved in the Wilbraham family, and was executed with sufficient care to be useful still to historians of London four hundred years later.

One of the more baffling aspects of Alley's work is the difficulty in knowing exactly why he wrote it or what purpose the 'litle booke' was intended to serve. The long and flowery dedicatory epistle to the current Lord Mayor, Sir Richard Saltonstall, and the pious sentiments addressed to the 'curteous reader' do little to enlighten us. The dedicatory epistle reads as if Alley believed that the Mayor and Alderman were not, perhaps, sufficiently aware of the various malpractices abroad in the City's markets and so he compiled the book to draw their attention to the widespread forestalling, regrating and engrossing which was being practised.[2] Alley, moreover, draws particular attention to the activities of hagglers, hawkers, hucksters and wanderers — the street traders of London — who bought up food in the markets and then took it away to sell, therby enhancing prices. It is these various malpractices which, Alley suggests, have lately 'bredd this great dearth and scarcety'. It is inconceivable, however, that the Lord Mayor and aldermen were not already aware of the problems of dearth and scarcity facing the City of London in the 1590s and the market offences detailed by Alley, while they may have aggravated the problems, certainly did not cause them.[3] Moreover, in spite of the verbosity of his writing Alley does not actually seem to be proposing any solution to the problems. His purpose in writing, and drawing, was to warn the Lord Mayor and aldermen about what was going on, to provide a *Caveat*. His solution, such as it was, seems to have been to urge the aldermen, and their deputies, in the wards in which the markets lay, to carry out the supervision of the markets with more care and attention, and to execute the city statutes which dealt with market offences with more rigour. Alley warns the Lord Mayor and aldermen about the widespread 'offences against penall lawes'. He writes that when he examined the markets of London he 'founde manye thinges of great moment cleane out of course and order' and so as a 'lovinge citizen' and loyal subject he decided to draw the attention of the City governors to the malpractices. His book is, therefore, in intention, essentially conservative rather than innovative: if the aldermen and their deputies would firmly execute the existing market 'penal laws' then all would be well. But although Alley's declared motives were loyalty and altruism, what we know about his career suggests that he may also have been hoping for employment by the Lord Mayor in the cause of market reform.[4] Alley asks Saltonstall to admit 'this smale worke ... and the author thereof into your patronage and protection'. Doubtless the Lord Mayors of the late sixteenth century received numerous *Caveats* of different kinds from disinterested citizens hoping thereby to secure employment, but few were likely to have been illustrated as Alley's was. Perhaps he was shrewd enough to realise that a different approach was needed to make his *Caveat* distinctive, and his ploy succeeded for in 1599 his schemes for market reforms were discussed by the Court of Aldermen and in September he was appointed to oversee the markets in order to prevent hucksters from buying up victuals in the markets for re-sale later.[5] This was one of the market offences to which Alley draws particular attention in the dedicatory epistle of the *Caveat*.

If Alley had no novel scheme for reform, then what is the purpose of the very intrusive, and clearly intentional, pillars which march across the market places of Alley's book? These pillars are of two kinds: in the common markets, i.e. those to which non-citizens came to sell victuals produced outside the city, Alley usually draws four or five pillars inscribed with the names of a county and surmounted by a flag.[6] In the case of the citizen markets, for example the Stocks or the Shambles, Alley draws only a single pillar, inscribed with one of the three major market offences, i.e. with the word 'Regrators' or 'Engrocers' or 'Forstallers' and again surmounted by a flag, usually the Royal Standard.[7] Attached to these single pillars are boards hanging from a hook by a rope. Was it Alley's intention that such pillars should be constructed and, if so, to what purpose? In the common markets the idea may have been that vendors from the named counties should cluster around the foot of 'their' pillar to sell their wares, although it is not clear how this would ensure better execution of the 'penal statutes'. In the case of the citizen markets the single pillar may have been intended to serve as a reminder to the vendors, of the City's regulations. Perhaps the hanging boards were to have written on them copies of the City's 'penal laws' or, perhaps, the names of convicted transgressors? There is, however, no evidence that such pillars were ever built in the market places of London. If it were not for the hanging boards on some of the pillars in the citizen markets, one might assume that the purpose of the pillars was merely to instruct the reader, that is to indicate particular malpractices which were prevalent in certain markets.

The booklet poses another question. To what extent is this little manuscript the work of Alley himself? There seems to be little doubt that the overall concept is his and that he wrote the text — such as it is — and copied it out. He asks the reader to excuse any faults and errors 'which hath passed my penne in writinge' but he then goes on to beg like indulgence for 'the paynter with his pensile in layenge cullours thereon'. Earlier in the letter to the courteous reader Alley wrote 'I have not desired to be curious, but plaine, with the poore painters pen and pensile, in colloringe and shaddowinge'. It seems likely that Alley himself not only wrote out his text (and his elaborate signature suggests that he was a man who enjoyed penman-ship)[8] but also executed the drawings both of the aldermen and their deputies, and of the markets and gates in pen and ink. A painter was then employed, however, to colour the drawings of the Lord Mayor, aldermen and deputies, and to 'shadow' the sketches of the markets.[9] The concept of the booklet is Alley's and he employed a painter to 'glamourise' his work and so make it more attractive and distinctive for presentation to the Lord Mayor and aldermen. The similarity of the poses of all the aldermen and their deputies, varying only in their distance apart on the page, suggests that Alley had a prototype which he copied with the result, as he himself confesses, that his figures are 'not soe neare to the lief of a man, yet to the countenance and habite of a man'. The treatment is varied somewhat for the Lord Mayor and the Swordbearer, but Alley has strayed as little as possible from the security of his prototype. There is not, moreover, a great deal of variety among the figures sitting in, or pacing through, the markets: here again Alley may have used prototypes from which to copy. The lady with the tall hat and a basket in her right hand appears in six of the pages,[10] and other characters appear more than once e.g. the lady sitting side-saddle on a horse, seen from behind.[11] The ships in the dock at Billingsgate look also as if they may have been taken from some other work, or a pattern book.[12] It seems likely that Alley had limited competence as an artist, but with the help, perhaps, of prototypes, or pattern books, he was able to insert figures (regardless of scale) into his drawings.

If one looks at the buildings in Alley's market drawings, one has the impression that here he is drawing freehand, either from memory, or observation, or both. He seems to decide what features are important to illustrate in the case of any particular market and then ensures that those are included regardless of scale; the rest is then made to fit in. In the case of Cheapside, the Cross and the Standard are given considerable prominence as, to a lesser extent, are the church of St Michael le Querne and the Great Conduit, but the Little Conduit outside St Michael's church, the streets running north out of Cheapside, and the notable buildings which lay on the north side of Cheapside, such as Mercers' Hall, are all ignored.[13] Alley knew his limitations. His drawings, therefore, of the markets are by no means comprehensive but, rather, selective. But where Alley does choose to portray a building, or feature, he does so with tolerable accuracy. We have, therefore, useful representations of the arcade of the market building at Billingsgate, the conduit in Gracechurch Street, the water-pump in the parish of St Andrew Undershaft, Leadenhall, the Stocks, the Cross, Standard and Great Conduit in Cheapside, the market houses at Southwark, Newgate and Queenhithe, and the pillory in Southwark. In the case of some of these buildings, Alley's drawings are the only representations of them which we have. The water-pump near Leadenhall had been set up as recently as 1576, but had to be rebuilt in 1602; the arcaded market houses at Newgate, Queenhithe and Southwark were all destroyed by fire in the later seventeenth century and then rebuilt. Alley has, therefore, preserved for us in visual form, as John Stow has in words, the outward appearance of buildings of which we would otherwise know nothing. The value of Alley's careful, if inexpert, work can be well demonstrated in the case of the Stocks market. The great stone market house known as the Stocks had been rebuilt in the early fifteenth century, and was later destroyed in the Great Fire of 1666. There are no visual representations of the building since, in the map views of 'Agas' and others, the market building is hidden behind St Mary Woolchurch. But the documentary evidence of the surviving deeds, together with Alley's drawing, has enabled Dr David Crouch to produce a convincing reconstruction of the lost building.[14] Without Alley's drawing this would not have been possible.

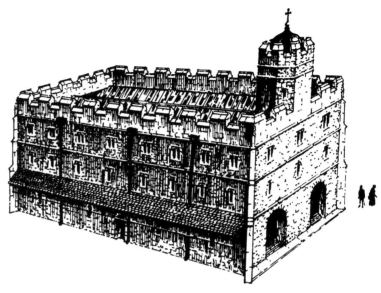

Figure 3
Reconstruction of the Stocks Market, c.1598, by David Crouch

There is some internal evidence to suggest how Alley set about his work. He conceived his book as an overall perambulation of the markets, i.e. he starts at London Bridge and moves through the markets of the City in an anti-clockwise direction, finally crossing the river to describe the Southwark Market. The route he follows is clear and logical.[15] What is also apparent is that he becomes less detailed, and less careful, in his drawings as the perambulation progresses: the houses become more schematic and less detailed; the people become fewer and fewer. Whereas in Billingsgate market Alley has drawn seven people, one dog and a variety of goods, in Queenhithe there are no people at all.[16] In New Fish Street market there are five people, three horses and a dog, and the fish laid out on the stallboards are drawn with considerable care, yet in Old Fish Street market there are only two people and a dog, and both the fish and the houses are drawn with much less care.[17] In the same way Eastcheap market is teeming with life: there are drovers, cattle, a dog and market women: the houses are given fretwork and finials and smoke from their chimneys and the joints of meat are carefully distinguished. The Shambles, by contrast, has only two people and the houses are perfunctory.[18]

But even if Alley clearly tired of his task, yet he completed it. As he wrote to the Lord Mayor 'for alwaies the good deede done is better then the good worke begonne and not fynished'. When Alley had completed the thirteenth, and last, drawing of the City's markets — Southwark — he found that he had five sides of his booklet left ready ruled for text or illustration. Rather than waste this space Alley decided to draw four of the City's gates showing country vendors passing through with their goods and packhorses. Although country people who had goods for sale would have had to pass through the City gates, and were there checked for toll, the control of the gates does not seem to have played a large part in schemes for market reform, or in the prevention of abuses in the marketing of victuals in London. It seems more likely that these tail-end drawings demonstrate Alley's artistic talent at its most free, and it is clear that he made little attempt to approximate his drawings of the city gates to the realities on the ground.

Although the drawings of the Lord Mayor, Swordbearer and aldermen follow a standard pattern, Alley has taken considerable trouble to portray their dress correctly. He must, therefore, have had some sort of access to the Court of Aldermen and knew, with accuracy, which of the aldermen had served as Mayor and which had not. His knowledge as to which alderman was serving which ward is extremely precise, and he knew about recent deaths.[19] Alley dated his work to 1598, but from details about the aldermen whom he depicts, it is possible to narrow down the date of composition. The work is addressed to Sir Richard Saltonstall, so it must have been written after Saltonstall was knighted in March 1598. The alderman shown for the ward of Farringdon Within is wearing a chain of office of an ex-Lord Mayor. This man must, therefore, be Richard Martin who moved, in 1598, to Bread Street ward, rather than his successor Humphrey Weld who had not yet served his turn as mayor. Weld was sworn at Farringdon Within on 9 May 1598, and so we may deduce that Alley completed his work in April 1598. In fact Alley gives us an accurate depiction of fourteen of the members of the Court of Aldermen in this month. Since the work was to be presented to the Lord Mayor and his brethren it is not surprising, perhaps, that Alley has shown their clothing with meticulous care. The colour plates reveal how carefully Alley instructed his painter. This fastidious representation of the dress of the aldermen,

Swordbearer, Lord Mayor and deputies (who were all Common Councilmen) lends Alley's work a unique value, and indicates how important to Elizabethan society was the outward and visible appearance of a man. Dress was often carefully controlled by society (by national legislation or by civic ordinance) and, if read aright, could reveal a man's place and standing within his community: no fine dress, no significant office.

Hugh Alley was born into a modest artisan family in Westminster and his life contained no meteoric rise to fame and fortune. He acquired some learning and clerkly skills: he made a modest living from rooting out abuses and taking his share of the fines paid by abusers.[20] There must have been many like him in late sixteenth century London, all jostling for the crumbs of attention and patronage which might fall from the tables of the wealthy aldermen and merchants of the City. Alley died in comparative poverty and obscurity and yet he managed to observe his own injunction 'to leave some remembrance behinde unto others which may hereafter performe and mayntaine the same'.

NOTES

[1] For a recent study of Treswell, see John Schofield, *The London Surveys of Ralph Treswell* (LTS, 1987).
[2] See above, p. 5.
[3] M. Power, 'London and the control of the "crisis" of the 1590s', *History*, 70 (1985).
[4] See above, pp. 15–16.
[5] See above, p. 15.
[6] E.g. ff. 13 and 21.
[7] E.g. ff. 14 and 16.
[8] See f. 6.
[9] See colour plates.
[10] See ff. 10, 11,13, 14, 16, 23.
[11] See ff. 12, 15.
[12] See f. 9.
[13] See f. 15.
[14] See f. 14 and figure 3.
[15] See Figure 1.
[16] Compare f. 9 with f. 20.
[17] Compare f. 10 with f. 19.
[18] Compare f. 11 with f. 16.
[19] It is true that Alley does not always know within which wards some markets lay, but these are usually rather tricky cases where the market straddled more than one ward; see ff. 11v, 16v, 18v.
[20] See above, p. 20–2.

f. 2

The Epistle Dedicatorie.

To the right honorable S[i]r Richard Saltonstall, Knight Lo[rd]
Maior of the Cittie of London. Hugh Alley Citizen and
Plaisterer of London, wissheth yo[u]r good Lordshipp
all prosperitie in this life, and in the worlde
to come, Everlasting Salvacion
in Jhesus Christe Our Lorde.

Havinge a desire *Right Honorable*, to see the state of this our
noble Ilande (as in the bowells whereof, all wee godes
people, haue our beinge, And wherein wee haue lived even
unto this present daie) The Cheife *Lanthorne* of Light, under
god, by whome wee are gouerned is our moste gracious and
dreade *Soueraigne Ladie Queen Elizabeth*, And her Ma[jes]tie,
by godes Sufferaunce, hath now made Choise and ellection
of yo[u]r *Lordshippe*, to Rule and governe, the Greate
Chamber, and princelie Roialtie of this her honorable Cittie
of *London*; That firste, godes glorie maie bee aduanced,
Secondlie *Justice* maie bee dulie and trulie executed; And
thirdlie, *Vice and Idlenes* utterlie overwhelmed and brought
to nothing: and her Ma[jes]tes Lovinge Subiects, within
the same Cittie, Carefullie regarded: The *Riche* in his
offences, to bee punished: and *Vertue*, and *Equitie* in the
meanest and poorest person to be aduaunced and maintained:

f. 2v

I haue presumed under yo[u]r honorable favoure, to sett
forthe this littell booke, called *The forewarninge of offences,
againste penall Lawes*: wherein is not onelie sett forthe The
true plott of everie *Markett*, within the Cittie of London &
Suburbs of the same, But also the persons of everie *Alderman*
and *Deputie* in everie of the wardes, belonginge to the
same, being appointed governours and Carefull lookers
thereunto; And the true imperfections of these faultes and
offences used within this honorable Cittie of longe and
many years unrefourmed: Nowe, your lordshippe beinge
cheife gouernour thereof, is nowe comitted into your
charge, viz: not onely, by diuerse Lewde, couetous, greedy,
and euill disposed people:

To the great offence of almightie god, and impouerishinge of
good citizens, and the best degree, of common sortes of her
ma[jestie]s lovinge subiects: in *forstallinge, Regratinge*, and
Engrossinge of all kinde of prouisions brought into all the said
marketts, and enhauncinge, and raysing uppe, of all prices,
of all kinde of wares and marchandizes, within the said
cittie: But also, by a sorte, of like greedie kinde of people,
inhabitinge in and about the citty, & suburbs of the same,
called *Haglers, Hawkers, Huxters*, and *wanderers*, uppe and
downe the streetes, in buyenge into their owne handes, to
rayse the prices, for their owne luker, and pryvate gayne, all
kinde of prouisions, and *victualls*, used and exercised, in the
same Cittie, to be bought, or solde, and presently sellinge
the same agayne to others in the same marketts, the
inconvenyenc[e] whereof, in these fewe late yeares, hath
bredd, this | great dearth and scarcety:

f. 3

To the great displeasure, of almightie god, and the utter ruyne,
and overthrowinge, of all the poorer sortes of people,
inhabitinge in and about the said cittye, and suburbes of the
same: And contrary to diuerse good, and wholsome lawes
and *statutes*, in that case made and provide: And for lack of
due ponishinge, the violaters and contemners, of the said
good and wholsome *statute*:

In all which the premisses, (*Right honorable*;) I nowe at this
tyme, obseruinge and lookinge, into euery markett, and
places of meetinges, of all sortes and disposicions of people
frequentinge to the same, I founde manye thinges, of greate
moment, cleane out of course and order:

And therefore, did bend my self, as a dutifull subiect, to her
ma[jes]tie: and servaunt to your *Lordshippe*, and a lovinge
citizen & member of the same to present this litle booke,
and my self, to the censure and good likinge, of your good
Lordshipp:

And thus, indeuoringe my self, to doe good, one for another, if
not to my self, yet to others, and that for conscience sake: yf
not for that, yet for the feare of god, and for the *Loyalty* of our
dutye, wee do all owe, as good and faithfull subiectes to her
ma[jes]tie, and loue to yo[u]r good L[ordshi]p:

lett us, while wee are here, liue to doe good deeds; & to leaue some remembrance behinde, unto others, w[hi]ch may hereafter performe and mayntaine the same: for alwaies, the good deede done, is better then the good worke begonne, and not fynished: Of these deepe consideracions I humble leaue them, to the graue regard, of your good *Lordship*:

f. 3v And therefore, to bend my stile, towards your *honor*, after I had [purposed *inserted*] in this sorte[, to *inserted*] publishe[d *deleted*], and set forth the same: I considered with my self, to whom I might dedicate the same: And after many aduisements had, *pro, et con*. I was at the laste, resolued to dedicate the same, rather to your honor, then to any other, and that for twoe causes: First, for that it hath pleased god to calle you (and that most worthely) to the *Regiment* of this soe famous, and populous a citty: to this end (noe doubt) that by the *sword* of authority, you might suppresse *vice*, and by the *Scepter* of wise gouerment, you maye comaunde, and enioyne men, to the practizing and setting forwarde, of this good deed, now in hand in this litle booke sett forth, to be by yo[u]r *Lordship*, and yo[u]r *right worshipfull Bretheren*, presently performed:

And not doubting, but the same hereafter, for euer wylbe continued, in this soe famous and *Honorable A citty*: whereunto, all nations under the *Heauens*, doth resorte. and the onely patterne, and *Eye* Looker, of this her ma[jestie]s realme of Englande:

All which good, and godlye deede, thus begonne, and finally ended, will noe doubt, please god, be liked of her ma[jes]tie, and her honorable Councell, and your *honorable good lordship* shall receaue imortal prayse, and good prayers, of all sortes of degrees, of good people:

Accepte therefore, my very good Lorde, according to your pristine *affability*, this smale worke, of myne, thus begunne, in yo[u]r *honors name*, and admit both it & the author f. 4 thereof, | into your patronage, and protection. *Soe* shall I thinke my self remunerate, and in happines, and shall daiely be bounde, to praye unto god, for the longe lief and prosperous continuance, of your good lordship, with all your right worshipfull Bretheren, cheif officers, & guides. of the charge comitted into their handes, in this honorable cittie: written from the harte and willing mynde, of a dutifull citizen, the [*blank*] daie of [*blank*], in the fortith yeare, of the raigne, of our moste gracious soueraigne, Ladie, queene Elizabeth: &c [*?*] 1598:

Your good *Lordships* in all dutifulnes,

Hugh Alley:

To the courteous Reader   f. 5

Consideringe with my selfe (gentle reader) the greate Decaye, or rather the playne abbolishm[en]t, and exterminacion of good deeds, often done unto others, and diuerse of them, for the most parte, very unthanckfull people. And there were neuer, more increase of them, then in these our daungerous and unhappie dayes:

I thought it most fittinge, for this present tyme, to publish, this Smale Booke, or plott of *Forwarninge of offences, against penall Lawes*: to the end, it might *stirre up* the mindes of some kinde of people, to carrie better consciences, and not to *Rack and Sacke*, all unto their owne greedie couetous purses and paunches: to the enrichinge of themselves, and impoauerishinge of their poore Neighbours, But upon lawfull Warninge to take good head, in Breach of the same Lawes:

The Argument (I appeale to thy conscience, in the feare of god) is good; the end and purpose of the Author also comendable.

And therefore, I doubt not, but it wilbe well liked, and also noe lesse esteemed of all that feare god. And then, for the likinge, or dislikinge, of others, I am so farre of for caringe for it; that I praye god, I maye neuer, neither saie, doe, nor wright, anye thinge, that may be liked, or applauded of them.

The Epistle Dedicatorie

f. 5v for the manner of the conceipte herof, I haue done it, in gods feare, and for the good, of this my natiue cuntrye and soyle, wherein I was bred, and borne: I haue not desired to be curious, but plaine, with the poore painters pen, and pensile, in colloringe and shaddowinge, the work of the same, euery one, acording to the nature of the place, where they be placed: And althoughe, not soe neare to the lief of a man, yet to the countenance, and habite of a man: And diuerse men, grauely shewinge their gestures and places:

I seeke not vaine glorie, nor worldly praise, (which many greene heades, make soe much accompt of.) but profit, to the behoulder hereof, and gaine to the poore, distressed sorte, of the people, of this honorable Citty, and all other like good cytties and townes, within this realme, which hereafter intendeth to follow, the same example:

And if there be any fault or Error, which hath passed my penne in writinge, or the paynter, with his pensile in layenge cullours thereon: I praye thee, in frendly kind manner, to let it passe, without findinge: And harteninge me, in this it will incorage me, to goe forward, in [the *deleted*] other like concept, to doe my cuntry, some more good hereafter:

And if thou reapest, any comodity of these my laboures, f. 6 Ascribe the glorie, to him, whom the heauens doe worship: the holye Angels doe reuerence, and the powers doe adore. And thus I comitt thee to god; and my Booke, to the Censure of the godly, and well disposed mindes, of good people, in gods feare, whersoeuer dispersed, ouer the face of the earth: &c. Thyne in the Lorde.

Hugh Alley:

'A CAVEATT FOR THE CITTY
OF LONDON'

A Caueatt for the Citty of London.

OR

A forewarninge of offences

against penall Lawes

1598

2

The Epistle Dedicatorie

To the right honorable Sr Richard Saltonstall, Knight Lo:
Maior of the Cittie of London, Hugh Alley Citizen and
Plaisterer of London wisheth yor good Lordshipp
all prosperitie in this life, and in the worlde
to come, Everlastinge Salvation
in Jhesus Christe our Lorde./

Hauinge, Adesire Right Honorable, to see the state of this our noble Jland (as, in the bowelles whereof, all wee goddes people, haue our beinge, And wherein, wee haue lived even vnto this present daie) The Chiefe Lanthorne of Light, vnder god, by whome wee are gouerned is our moste gracious and dreade Soueraigne Ladie Queene Elizabeth; And her ma^{tie}, by goddes sufferannce, hath now made choise and ellection, of yor Lordshippe, to Rule and gouerne, the Greate Chamber, and princelie Roialtie of this her honorable Cittie of London; That firste, goddes glorie maie bee aduanced, Secondlie Justice maie bee dulie and trulie executed; And thirdlie, Vice and Jdlenes vtterlie overwhelmed and broughtt to nothinge; and her ma^{tie} lovinge Subiecte, within the same Cittie, maie fullie regarded: The Riche, in his offences, to bee punished: and Vertue, and Equitie in the meanest and poorest person to bee aduanced and maintained:/

'A Caveatt for the Citty of London'   f.2v

The Epistle Dedicatorie

I haue presumed vnder yo.r honorable fauoure, to sett forthe this litttle booke, called. The forewarninge of offences, againste penall Lawes: wherein is not onelie sett forthe the true plott of euerie Markett, within the Cittie of London & Suburbs of the same, But also the persons of euerie Alderman and Deputie, in euerie of the wardes, belonginge to the same; being appointed gouernours and carefull lookers there vnto; And the true imperfections of these faultes and offences vsed within this honorable Cittie of longe and many yeares vnreformed: Nowe, your lord= shippe beinge cheife gouernour thereof, is nowe comitted into your charge, viz: not onely, by & diuerse Lewde, routous, greedy, and euill disposed people.

To the greate offence of almightie god, and impouerishinge of good citizens, and the best degree, of comon sortes of her ma.ts louinge subiectts: In forstallinge, Regratinge, and Engrossinge, of all kinde of prouisions brought into all the said markettes, and enhauncinge, and raysing vppe, of all prices, of all kinde of wares and marchandizes, within the said cittie: But also, by a sorte, of like greedie kinde of people, inhabitinge, in and aboute, the citty & suburbs of the same, called Haglers, Hawkers, Huxters, and wanderers, vppe and downe the streetes, in buyenge into their owne handes, to rayse the prices, for their owne luker, and pryuate gayne, all kinde of prouisions, and victualls, vsed and exercised, in the same cittie, to be bought, or solde, and presently sellinge the same agayne to others, in the same markettes, the inconuenyent whereof, in these fewe late yeares, hath bredd this

The Epistle Dedicatorie

greate dearth, and scarsety:

To the greate displeasure, of almightie god, and the vtter ruyne, and overthrowinge, of all the poorer sortes of people, inhabitinge, in and aboute the said cittye, and suburbes of the same: And contrary, to diuerse good, and wholsome lawes and Statutes, in that case made and prouided: And for lack of due ponishinge, the violaters and contemners, of the said good & wholsome Statute:

In all which, the premisses, (Right honorable:) I nowe at this tyme, observinge and lookinge, into euery markett, and places of meetinges, of all sortes, and dispositions of people, frequentinge to the same, I founde manye thynges, of greate moment, cleane out of course & order:

And therefore, did bend my selfe, as a dutifull subiect, to her Ma:tie and servaunt to your Lordshippe, and a lovinge citizen member of the same, to present this litle booke, and my selfe, to the censure and good likinge, of your good Lordshipp:/

And thus indeuoringe my selfe, to doe good, one for another, if not to my selfe, yet to others, and that for conscience sake: yf not for that, yet for the feare of god, and for the Loyaltye, of our dutye, wee doe all owe, as good and faithfull subiectes to her Ma:tie, and loue to ye good L: P: &

lett vs, while wee are here liue, to doe good deeds; to leaue, some remembrance behynde, vnto others, wch may, hereafter pforme and mayntaine the same: ffor alwaies, the good deede done, is better then the good worke begonne, and not fynished: Of these deepe consideratons: I humbly, leaue them, to the graue regard, of your good Lordship:

The epistle dedicatorie

And therefore, to bend my stile, towardes your honor, after I had, in this sorte, *purposed,* publishe, and
set forth the same: I consjdered with my selfe, to whome I might dedicate the same:~
And after many aduisements had, pro, et con: It was at the laste, resolued, to dedicate
the same, rather to your honor, then to any other, and that for twoe causes: First, for
that it hath, pleased god, to calle you (and that moste worthely,) to the Regiment,
of this soe famous, and populous a citty; to this end (noe donbt,) that by the
sword of authority, you might suppresse vice, and by the Scepter, of wise gou
ment, you maye remannde, and enioyne, men, to the practizinge, and settinge for
warde, of this good deede, nowe in hande, in this litle booke sett forth,) to be by yor
Lordship, and yor right worshipfull Bretheren, presently performed :/

And not doubtinge, but the same hereafter, for euer wylbe continued, in this soe famous,
and Honorable A citty: wherevnto, all nations vnder the Heauens, doth resorte.
and the onely patterne, and Eye looker, of this her maties realme of Englande :/

All which good, and godlye deede, thus begonne, and finally ended, will noe donbt, please
god, be liked of her matie, and her honorable coumsell and your honorable good Lordship, &
shall receaue, mortall prayse, and good prayers, of all sortes, of degrees, of good people :

Accepte therefore, my very good Lorde, accordinge to your pristine affability. this smale
worke, of myne, thus begunne, in yor honors name, and admitt both it, & the author thereof

4

The Epistle Dedicatorie

into your patronage, and protection. Soe shall I, thinke my selfe, remunerate, and in happines,
and shall daicly, be bonnde, to praye vnto god, for the longe liefe. and prosperous continuance,
of your good Lordship, with all your right worshipfull Bretheren, cheif officers, & guydes,
of the charge comitted, into their handes, in this honorable citties: written from the harte
and willinge mynde, of a dutifull citizen, the   daie of   in the fortith
yeare, of the raigne, of our moste gracious souvraigne, Ladie, queene Elizabeth: Anno 1598.

                    Your good Lordships in all dutifulnes

Hughe: Alley:

5

TO the curteous Reader

CONSIDERINGE with my selfe (gentle reader) the greate Decaye, or rather, the playne abbolishmt, and exterminacōn, of good deedes, often done vnto others, and diuerse of them, for the most parte, very vnthanckfull people. And there were neuer, more increase of them, then in these, our soe daungerous and vnhappie dayes:

J thought it most fittinge, for this present tyme, to publish, this smale Booke, or plott, of fforwarninge off offences, against penall lawes: to the end, it might stirre vp, the mindes of some kinde of people, to carrie better consciences, and not to Rack, and Sacke, all vnto their owne, greedie, couetous, purses, and paunches: to the enrichinge of themselues, and impouerishinge, of their poore Neighbours, But vpon lawfull warninge: to take good head, in breach of the same Lawes :

The, Argument (J appeale to thy conscience, in the feare of god) is good; the end and purpose of the Author also, comendable :

And therefore, J doubt not, but it wilbe well liked, and also noe lesse esteemed, of all that feare god. And then, for the likinge, or dislikinge, of others: J am soe farre of, for carninge for it: That J praye god, J maye neuer, neither saie, doe, nor wright, anye thinge, that maye be liked, or applauded of them:

To the Curteous Reader

for the manner of the conceipte herof. J haue done it, in gods feare, and for the good of this my natiue cuntrye, and soyle, wherein J was bred, and borne: J haue not desi=red to be curious, but plaine, with the poore painters pen, and pensile, in colloringe and shaddowinge the work of the same, euery one, according to the nature of the place, where they be placed: And althoughe, not soe neare, to the lief of a man, yet to the countenance, and habite of a man: And diuerse men, grauely shewinge their gestures and places:

J seeke not vaine glorie, nor worldly praise, (which many greene heades, make so much accompt of) but profit, to the behoulder hereof, and game to the poore distressed sorte, of the people, of this honorable Citty, and all other, like good cytties, and townes, within this Realme, which hereafter, intendeth to followe, the same example:

And if there be, any fault or Error, which hath passed my penne, in writinge or the paynter, with his pensile in layenge cullours, thereon. J praye thee, in frendly kinde manner, to let it passe, without findinge: And harteninge me, in this it will incourage me, to goe forward, in the other the like conceipt, to doe my cuntry, some more good hereafter:

6

To the Curteous Reader

And if thou reapest any comodity by these my laboures, Ascribe the glorie, to him, whom the heauens doe worship: The holye Angels doe reuerence, and the powers doe adore. And thus I comitt the, to god; and my Baoke, to the Censure of the godly, and well disposed mindes, of good people, in gods feare, wher-soeuer dispersed, ouer the face of the earth: &

Thyne in the Lorde.

'A Caveatt for the Citty of London' f.8

8

'A Caveatt for the Citty of London'   f.9

BRIDGE WITHIN:

CANDELWEEKE STREETE

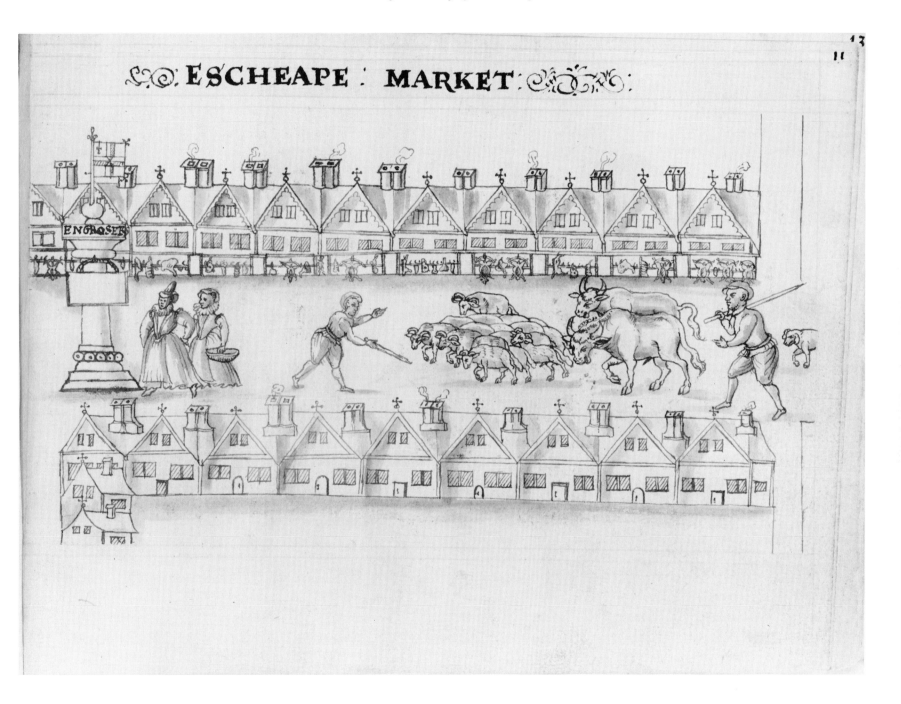

'*A Caveatt for the Citty of London*'   *f.11v*

'A Caveatt for the Citty of London'   f.12

'A Caveatt for the Citty of London' f.12v

LYME STREETE

BRODE STETE

14

'A Caveatt for the Citty of London' f.14v

CHEAPE WARDE

7

'A Caveatt for the Citty of London' f.15v

FARRINGTON WITHIN

'A Caveatt for the Citty of London'   f.16v

'A Caveatt for the Citty of London' f.17

'A Caveatt for the Citty of London'   f.17v

ᛕ᛫FARRINGTON᛫WITHOVT᛫ᛕ

18

SMITHFELD

ENGROCERS

'A Caveatt for the Citty of London'   f.19

QVEENE·HiTHE·WARDE·

20

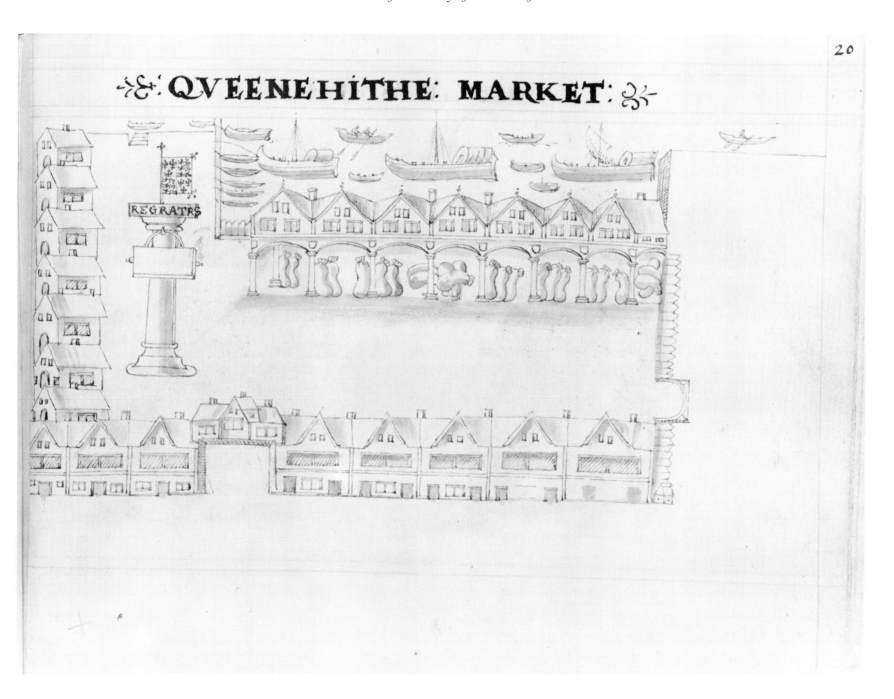

BRIDGE WITHOVT:

'A Caveatt for the Citty of London'   f.21

'A Caveatt for the Citty of London'   f.21v

BISSHOPES GATE

22

⌇: LVDGATE :⌇

⚞:ALGATE⚟

23

COMMENTARY

f. 8 [The Lord Mayor and Swordbearer] Plate I and p. 51.

The Lord Mayor shown on the left is Sir Richard Saltonstall (knighted *c.*March 1598) who came from Halifax and had made a successful career in the city as a skinner and Merchant Adventurer. He was much involved with government policy in the Low Countries and provided money and exchange facilities to assist the English cause there in the 1580s and 1590s. By December 1598, just a few months after this drawing was made, he was described as 'old and sickly' so that his son Samuel was allowed to collect the customs as his deputy. Saltonstall died in 1601 and was buried at South Ockendon in Essex where he had built up a considerable country estate. After his death his will was disputed among his seven sons, nine daughters and one illegitimate daughter.[1]

The robes of the Lord Mayor are very carefully portrayed and this reflects the considerable attention which was paid at this time to the attire of the mayor and aldermen.[2] The Mayor is shown here wearing a scarlet gown trimmed with fur. On other occasions he might wear a violet gown and in summer these gowns would be trimmed with taffeta rather than fur. In the same way the cloaks worn by the mayor and aldermen were subject to regulation: between Michaelmas and Whitsun the cloaks were to be of violet and furred, and from Whitsun to Michaelmas simply of scarlet. By 1604 it was further specified that the Lord Mayor and those aldermen who had served as mayor were to have their cloaks lined with 'gray amis' and those aldermen who had not been mayor were to line their cloaks with 'calavse'.[3] Both of these were squirrel furs, but 'amys grey' were the expensive dressed winter skins of the grey squirrel from the Baltic whereas 'calabre' were the less valuable white belly skins from Calabria. Saltonstall is clearly wearing a winter cloak of violet lined with rich 'gray amis'.

The mayoral chain which Saltonstall is shown wearing is a collar of SS bequeathed in 1545 to the City by Sir John Aleyn, mercer and ex-Lord Mayor, 'to be used always and worn by the Lord Mayor of this City for the time being'.[4] In 1558 Sir Martin Bowes gave the jewel which was to hang from the chain and this was described as a 'cross of gold with diverse precious stones and pearls'.[5] It must be the Bowes jewel which Alley has shown

hanging from Saltonstall's chain, but it is not, perhaps, very accurately delineated. The jewel was again described in a City inventory of 1632/3 as of 'fair raised work and enamelled with gold added therunto, having a great emerald and two sapphires moon fashion with a great ballast three pointed diamond and four great pearls'. In fact this sumptuous jewel had been replaced by a yet more magnificent one in 1607.[6]

The Swordbearer shown here is Rowland Smart, a mercer, who had succeeded Matthew Sturdevant in the office in 1591. The Swordbearer's office had grown in importance since its origins in the late fourteenth century. By 1552 the Swordbearer had authority over all members of the Lord Mayor's household and, in effect, ran the household and controlled the flow of petitions to the Lord Mayor.[7] He was provided with a servant and a house, usually over one of the city gates. The Swordbearer attended the Mayor daily and carried the sword before him whenever he moved around the city, as Alley here shows. Rowland Smart clearly carried out his duties very well for in September 1596 it had been decided that he should receive an annual payment of £25 p.a. (instead of the usual £20) over and above the normal fee and salary paid to the Swordbearer. In 1606 it was decided that this £25 was to be paid not during pleasure, but for Smart's natural life, and two years later he was paid a £3 housing allowance even though he was provided with a house over Bishopsgate. Smart remained in office until 1619.[8]

The Swordbearer was provided, at the City's expense, with a gown of damask trimmed and faced with velvet and also with eight coats of russet cloth garded (i.e. trimmed), with russet velvet.[9] It would seem to be one of these everyday coats which Alley depicts here, and the velvet ribbon trimming is clearly shown. The Swordbearer wears only a gown, without a cloak.

The City also provided the Swordbearer with a hat. In 1519 it was decided that the Swordbearer's hat should be 'of the most goodliest fashion devised' and in 1520 the 'goodliest fashion' was decided to be grey fur in winter and silk in summer. In 1546 the Lord Mayor gave a 'very goodly and rich hat for the swordbearer' and this may have been kept for special occasions when the Swordbearer wore his damask gown.[10] By the early seventeenth century the Swordbearer's 'rich hat' was made of crimson velvet and was known as the 'cap of maintenance'.[11] This 'rich hat' does not, however, seem to be that shown by Alley for here Smart is shown wearing a plain stiff hat of a golden brown colour, perhaps made of silk. It is clearly not the formal cap of maintenance, nor is it made of fur, although it is carefully drawn and distinguished from the soft black velvet hats worn by the mayor and aldermen.

The Swordbearer is carrying before the Lord Mayor one of the City's swords. Several splendid swords were given to the City in the middle of the sixteenth century, one by Sir Ralph Warren in 1545 which had a rich scabbard of crimson velvet garnished with gold, and another by Richard Matthew, cutler, in 1563, also with a crimson scabbard 'well garnished'.[12] Smart could be carrying either of these. The swords, with their scabbards, were in constant use, being carried around the city by the Swordbearer, and so they often became 'old and unfitting to be carried any longer'. So the swords, and in particular the scabbards, had frequently to be remade.[13] Although on state occasions the City's sword was sheathed in a scabbard of gold tissue decorated with pearls, it was the crimson velvet scabbard which was provided for daily use and this is the scabbard which Smart is here shown holding erect before the Mayor.[14]

NOTES

[1] *H of C*, iii, pp. 335–6; Beaven, ii, p. 43.

[2] Small handbooks dealing with 'The ordre of my Lorde Mayor, the Aldermen and shireffes for their meetings and wearing of theyr apparell throughout the yeare' appear from 1568 onwards and may have been produced annually. There is a copy of the 1568 pamphlet in the Huntington Library in California (photostat copy in Guildhall Library, ref. Pam. 7971) and a copy of the 1604 version in Guildhall Library, ref. A.8.1. no. 21.

[3] Ibid., 1604 edition, p. 11.

[4] CLRO Rep. 11, f. 215, and see Llewellyn Jewitt, *The Corporation Plate and Insignia of the office of the cities and towns of England and Wales*, with large additions by W. St John Hope, II (1859), pp. 111–14. In 1568 the Aleyn collar was enlarged.

[5] Ibid., p. 114, citing CLRO Rep. 14, f. 99v.

[6] CLRO City Cash I: 1625–35, f. 95.

[7] T. Kingsley Collett, 'The Swordbearer' in *Transactions of the Guildhall Historical Association*, 3 (1963), pp. 39–45; see also Betty R. Masters, 'The Mayor's Household before 1600' in A. E. J. Hollaender and W. Kellaway (eds.), *Studies in London History presented to P. E. Jones* (1969), pp. 95–114.

[8] CLRO, Rep. 22, f. 251; 23, f. 582v; 27, f. 285v; 28, f. 313v.

[9] Jewitt, *Corporation Plate*, p. 108. Cf. CLRO Rep. 18, f. 407; 19, f. 411v; 21, f. 489v.

[10] Jewitt, *Corporation Plate*, pp. 101, 108.

[11] In 1614 Rowland Smart was paid £4 18s. for his costs in having the hat of crimson velvet known as the 'cap of maintenance' repaired, CLRO Rep. 31 (ii), f. 391.

[12] Jewitt, *Corporation Plate*, pp. 101–3.

[13] Jewitt, *Corporation Plate*, pp. 103–4. In 1603 Smart was paid 42s. 11d. for new scabbards, and again in 1615: CLRO, Rep. 26 (i), f. 151; 32, ff. 216v, 248.

[14] A third scabbard provided for the city sword was of black velvet and used in times of mourning.

f. 8v   BILLINGESGATE WARDE   p. 52

The Alderman of Billingsgate ward, shown on the right, was Thomas Lowe, a haberdasher, who had not yet served as mayor, hence the absence of a chain. He was to be mayor of London in 1604–5 and was then to be elected as the City's MP to three later Parliaments. He served for long periods as president of St Bartholomew's Hospital and as a governor of the Levant Company. He died in 1623.[1] Like all the aldermen in Alley's drawings he is shown wearing a scarlet gown trimmed with fur, but without a cloak.

The man on the left is the alderman's deputy. The deputy was, in many respects, the lynch pin of local government in the City: mayoral precepts were almost always addressed to the alderman, or his deputy. He was chosen by a process of negotiation and agreement at the wardmote between the good men and the alderman of the ward. Whereas in the fifteenth century the appointment of a deputy was casual and ad hoc, depending largely on whether the alderman was able to exercise his duties or not, by the mid sixteenth century it is clear that the Court of Aldermen assumed that every alderman would have a deputy. He was usually the senior common councilman of the ward. There are no surviving lists of deputies and so our knowledge of them depends upon chance references in civic or parish records.[2]

Deputies usually resided in the wards, whereas aldermen frequently did not, hence to the deputy fell much of the routine business of ward administration. Most of the men who served as deputies in the second half of the sixteenth century came from the upper ranks of urban society, but were not sufficiently prosperous, or successful, to serve as aldermen. They were usually middling merchants, or large-scale retailers. The important role of the deputy in the ward is well reflected in

Alley's depiction of him stepping out purposefully alongside his alderman to prevent breaches of market regulations. It is likely that it would, in fact, be the deputy rather than the alderman upon whom the main burden of overseeing the markets within the ward would fall.[3] But his subordinate position is reflected in his clothing. Whereas the Alderman wears a scarlet (or violet) gown, common councilmen wore grey gowns and were often referred to as 'grey gowns' or 'grey cloaks'.[4] But although the gown was grey, it was trimmed with fur like that of the alderman.

The man shown here is probably John Archer who was serving as deputy for Billingsgate ward in 1599. He was a fishmonger and master of the company in 1594. He had served as a Common Councilman since 1583 and had also been a governor of St Thomas's Hospital. He served on numerous city committees and was nominated as a Bridgemaster in 1598. Archer lived at Fresh Wharf in the parish of St Botolph Billingsgate.[5]

NOTES

[1] Beaven, ii, p. 45.

[2] This paragraph, and the following one, are based upon Caroline M. Barron, 'The Government of London and its relations with the Crown 1400–1450' (unpublished London PhD thesis, 1970, p. 72), and Ian W. Archer, 'Governors and Governed in late Sixteenth-Century London *c*.1560 to 1603: studies in the achievement of stability' (Oxford D.Phil. thesis, in progress).

[3] By the terms of the Act of Common Council of February 1600, inspired by Alley's proposals, the overseers of the markets were instructed to report on market offences to the alderman, *or his deputy* (my italics), CLRO, Journal 25, f. 151.

[4] See, for example, 'The Ordre of My Lord Mayor' (1568 edn), p. 10v.

[5] Benbow, Index.

---

f. 9 BILLINGESGATE p. 53

Billingsgate quay is seen here from the west. Billingsgate was originally a gate in London's riverside wall, but by 1337, and probably earlier, it was a dock where ships were unloaded. Since it lay downstream of London Bridge it became increasingly more frequented than Queenhithe (see f. 20), and it was easier for larger ships to tie up there. The arcade which is so prominent a feature of the dock in Alley's drawing is also to be found on other depictions of Billingsgate (e.g. the famous

miniature drawn *c*.1490 for the poems of Charles, duke of Orleans, BL MS Royal 16 F.ii, f. 73 and Wyngaerde's panorama of *c*.1540).[1] This open arcade probably served as a storage place for goods after they were unloaded. The arcade was surmounted by two further storeys, not shown by Alley, but clearly depicted in the other representations. This impressive arcaded building may, perhaps, be dated to the middle of the fifteenth century. In 1449 the City bought lands from the executors of Sir Thomas Haseley for £1,000 to extend Billingsgate.[2]

Although goods may have been unloaded and stored in the covered arcade, the actual market appears to have been held in the railed open space to the north of the dock, known as Romeland. In the 1520s, and again in the 1540s, the City had to dispute the ownership of the open space at Billingsgate with the parish of St Mary at Hill, but Henry VIII, by a decree in Chancery, declared in 1545 that the open space to the north of Billingsgate belonged to the citizens of London, on which they had held a market, time out of mind.[3]

The small house shown by Alley within the railed market area may be the boss, or fresh water fountain, which was originally constructed here by the executors of Richard Whittington (d. 1423).[4]

In 1559 it was decided that Billingsgate should be an open place appointed for the landing or bringing in of fish, corn, salt, stones, victuals and fruits, but not grocery wares.[5] Stow comments that the ships and boats which arrived at Billingsgate commonly brought in fresh fish, oranges, onions and other fruits and roots, wheat, rye and other grains. Most of these commodities can be identified in the hands, or on the backs, of the people whom Alley has drawn in the foreground.[6] The seated woman on the left is holding a type of scales in common use at this period.

NOTES

[1] See John Schofield, *The Building of London from the Conquest to the Great Fire* (1984), frontispiece and p. 122.

[2] Caroline M. Barron, 'Government of London', p. 226.

[3] CCPR, Billingsgate. The area was known as Romeland by 1421: Harben, pp. 506–7.

[4] Stow, i, p. 208.

[5] Dietz, p. 158.

[6] Stow, i, p. 206.

f. 9v BRIDGE WITHIN p. 54

The Alderman, on the right, is Roger Clarke, a salter. He had only been elected as alderman in the previous year and he did not serve as sheriff until 1599. He held comparatively few City offices, ceased to be an alderman in 1605 and died three years later.[1]

Clarke's deputy, shown on the left, seems to have been a much more notable Londoner. He was probably Thomas Fettiplace, an ironmonger, who was certainly serving in 1599. He was prominent in his own company, serving as warden, and then as master, and he appears as a common councilman for Bridge ward in 1590 and subsequently served on some seventy committees, including the powerful City Lands committee in 1594–5. He was also a governor of Bridewell from 1589–1601. In 1597–8 he sat as an MP for London, and again in 1601 and he also served on numerous committees of the House and made many speeches on both occasions. Although he lived until 1618, he never became an alderman. He served as a churchwarden and auditor of his parish church of St Benet Gracechurch in the ward of Bridge, but by the time of his death in 1618 he had moved to the parish of St Botolph Billingsgate. He married twice, had three children and left land at Corringham in Essex.[2]

NOTES

[1] Beaven, ii, p. 46.
[2] *H of C*, ii, pp. 115–16; Benbow, Index.

f. 10 NEWE FISHESTREETE p. 55

The market is seen here from the west. New Fish Street ran northwards from London Bridge and was also known as Bridge Street; in fact the name New Fish Street occurs for the first time in 1545. The street is now known as Fish Street Hill.[1] A fishmarket was held here from the twelfth century and Stow wrote that 'in new Fishstreete bee Fishmongers and fayre Tavernes'.[2] Alley has clearly depicted the fishmongers with their stalls on which their wares are displayed, set up outside their houses.

To the right of the drawing, at the southern end of the street, Alley has shown Thames Street running to east and west. The road running west off New Fish Street, on the left hand side of the picture, may well be Crooked Lane.

Alley appears to have drawn two churches. A fraction of the battlemented tower of St Magnus is shown at the south-east corner of the junction of Thames Street and New Fish Street. Rather more of the church of St Margaret is shown to the left of the picture, with a crenellated tower surmounted by a bulbous cupola. Such a cupola is not shown on the copperplate map of *c*.1559.[3] Alley does, however, seem to show the footway that 'passeth by the south side of this church', which led from New Fish Street to Rother Lane (also known as Pudding Lane). St Margaret's Church had few monuments in Stow's day and was not rebuilt after the Great Fire.[4]

NOTES

[1] Harben, p. 232; *HTA* Gazetteer, under 'Newe Fysshestrete'.
[2] Stow, i, p. 211.
[3] *A–Z*, CP 2.
[4] Stow, i, p. 212.

f. 10v CANDELWEEKE STREETE p. 56

The alderman, on the right, is Sir Henry Billingsley, who had been knighted the previous year after serving as mayor. Since he had served as mayor he was entitled to wear a gold chain which Alley has accurately depicted. Billingsley was unusual among London merchants in having attended both Cambridge and Oxford universities, although he obtained no degree in either place. In 1570 he translated and published the first English version of Euclid's *Elements of Geometry*, and was also, perhaps on the strength of this work, a member of the Society of Antiquaries, founded by Archbishop Parker in 1572. He became an alderman in 1585 and then transferred from Tower to Candlewick Street in 1592 where he remained until his death. Billingsley married twice and had a large family: he set up his eldest son Henry (knighted 1603) in a manor house at Liston in Gloucestershire, but he himself died in London and was buried, in 1606, in the church of St Katharine Coleman. Like most of his contemporary aldermen, he did not live in his ward. He left bequests to the poor of his parish and endowed three scholarships at St John's College, Cambridge.[1]

The deputy in Candlewick ward at this time was Robert Thomas, a draper, who served from 1592 to 1602. He was a warden of his company and also served as a governor of St Thomas's Hospital. He lived in the ward, in the parish of St Martin Orgar, although in 1602, when he ceased to be deputy, he moved away from the ward to the parish of St Nicholas (probably in Queenhithe ward). He died in 1610.[2]

NOTES

[1] Beaven, ii, p. 42; *DNB*.
[2] Benbow, Index.

f. 11 ESCHEAPE MARKET p. 57

The market shown here is seen from the south. Eastcheap (also known as Great Eastcheap and Little Eastcheap) was the name used at various times to describe different portions of the long street which ran eastwards from Candlewick Street to Tower Street.[1] Alley is probably depicting the section running between St Michael's Lane, shown on the left hand side of the picture, and New Fish Street shown on the right.

Eastcheap was one of the City's 'flesh markets' and butchers lived on both sides of the street. Originally there were cook shops interspersed among the butchers, and also 'such other as solde victuals readie dressed of all sorts'.[2] But by the time that Stow was writing, and Alley was drawing, the cook shops had given way to uninterrupted rows of butchers' shops. Alley's picture would suggest that the butchers brought their meat to Eastcheap on the hoof and slaughtered the animals in, or near, their shops. Stow described how the butchers who lived at the eastern end of Eastcheap kept scalding houses for hogs and the 'puddings with other filth of beastes' were voided down Pudding Lane to dung boats on the Thames.[3] Alley spares us the details of the slaughter houses but shows the carcasses and joints hanging up on poles across the open shops (as today). The butchers' wares seem to be displayed inside, whereas the fishmongers of New Fish Street laid their goods out on shutter trestles in front of their shops.

NOTES

[1] Harben, pp. 211–13.
[2] Stow, i, p. 216.
[3] Ibid., pp. 210–11; P. E. Jones, *The Butchers of London* (1976), pp. 83, 87–9.

f. 11v Untitled p. 58

Alley does not name this ward but it would seem, in fact, to be Bishopsgate since most of Gracechurch Street lay within this ward. It is true, however, that the street actually straddled three wards, Bishopsgate, Bridge, and Langborne, and Alley may have been uncertain to which alderman to allocate responsibility for the Gracechurch Street market. Since only a very small part of Gracechurch Street lay within Langborne ward, and the alderman of Bridge had another market for which he was responsible, it seems likely that Alley had the alderman of Bishopsgate in mind.

In fact the alderman of Bishopsgate ward at this time was William Thwayte, a fishmonger. He had only been elected alderman in the previous year and was currently serving as Prime Warden of the Fishmongers' Company, but he died in the autumn of 1598 and so had a truncated civic career.[1]

Bishopsgate ward had two deputies, probably because it straddled the city wall. One of the deputies serving at this time was Thomas Armstrong, a tallowchandler. He had been a common councilman since 1573 and had been deputy since 1585. He served three times as warden, and twice as master, of his company. He lived in the parish of St Botolph Bishopsgate and served the local community as vestryman, auditor, constable, and churchwarden.[2]

NOTES

[1] Beaven, ii, p. 46.
[2] Benbow, Index.

f. 12 GRACE CHURCHE MARKET p. 59

The market here is viewed from the west. Gracechurch Street continued the line of New Fish Street northwards to the intersection with Cornhill. Alley depicts Fenchurch Street

Commentary

extending eastwards from Gracechurch Street with the little church of St Benet Gracechurch at the junction of the two streets. Both on the copperplate map of *c*.1559 and the 'Agas' map of *c*.1562 the church is shown with considerably more of a tower than is depicted here.[1]

The building on the right of Alley's drawing seems to be the conduit which was built by the executors of Sir Thomas Hill (mayor 1484–5) in 1491 and completed regardless of cost. Stow described the building as 'one fayre conduit of sweete water castellated with crest and vent'.[2] The conduit, with a small tower in one corner as Alley shows, appears also on the copper-plate map.[3]

Gracechurch market was an open market in the sense that vendors and producers from outside the city (here Middlesex, Essex, Kent and Surrey are specified) could come here to sell their goods. Although in the fourteenth century the market on the pavement at Gracechurch was primarily for cornmongers (especially those from the eastern counties) by the sixteenth century, it was a general market, where 'women, market folks and victuallers ... who come from outside the city' sold their goods. Such people were allowed to sell butter, cheese, fruit and other victuals as well as veal, pork and bacon but not beef or lamb.[4] The country vendors depicted by Alley appear to be selling fruit and vegetables, pig's trotters and heads, bacon, and sausages.

NOTES

[1] *A–Z*, 25, CP 2.
[2] Stow, i, pp. 110, 211; ii, p. 178.
[3] *A–Z*, CP 2.
[4] See above p. 10; CLRO, Letter Book Q, f. 186.

f. 12v LYME STREET p. 60

The alderman shown on the right is Sir John Harte, a grocer. He had already served as mayor and so wears a chain. He had served the City in many capacities and at the time that Alley depicted him he was surveyor-general of the City's hospitals. Harte came from Coxwold in Yorkshire where he founded a free school, and he became a very rich and successful merchant with a fine London town house, once the property of the earl of

Oxford, in the parish of St Swithin. Harte was a member of the Muscovy Company and was involved in overseas trade as well as in the domestic grocery trade.[1] He lent money to the aristocracy and bought land in Yorkshire, Lincolnshire, Essex, and Sussex. He was twice elected MP for the city and was active on Parliamentary committees. When he died in 1604 he left money to Sidney Sussex College, Cambridge, for the library and to establish a lectureship in Greek as well as exhibitions for undergraduates. His will is said to display 'Puritan overtones'.[2]

It has not been possible to discover who was the deputy for Lime Street ward in 1598.

NOTES

[1] See R. G. Lang, 'London's Aldermen in Business 1600–1625', *Guildhall Miscellany*, 3 (1971), pp. 242–64 esp. pp. 243, n. 6; 249, n. 57; 259, n. 131.
[2] *H of C*, ii, pp. 264–5; Beaven, ii, p. 41.

f. 13 LEADEN HALL MARKET p. 61

The Leadenhall building, and market held outside, are shown from the north. This street, which ran along the north side of Leadenhall, was known by 1605 as Leadenhall Street. In the sixteenth century it seems to have been known simply as 'the High Street'.[1]

On the left hand side of Alley's drawing (i.e. to the east) the artist depicts a water pump. This had been set up recently, in 1576, at considerable expense to the parish of St Andrew Undershaft, but it had to be renewed in 1602.[2]

Leadenhall market was, in fact two separate markets: the oldest one, shown in the foreground of Alley's drawing, was an open air street market for vendors of country produce; the covered market built by the City in the mid-fifteenth century can be seen behind the pillars in Alley's drawing. The quadrangular Leadenhall building which served also as a city granary, and contained a chapel, was probably arcaded at ground floor level and this would have been where the covered market was held. Alley does not show arcading but, rather, a kind of shuttering on which, perhaps, goods were displayed on market days.[3] Although in the fifteenth century Leadenhall had been used as a market for poultry and victuals, lead, nails, worsted cloth and leather, it is not clear that it was used so extensively for marketing by the second half of the sixteenth century. Stow describes how in his youth, the north range of the Leadenhall quadrangle housed the common beam for weighing wool on the east side of the north gate, and the scales for weighing meal on the west side. The remaining three sides of the quadrangle were used for storing sacks of wool and the City's pageant gear.[4] It is clear, however, that in the 1590s meal, leather, and meat were sold in the Leadenhall building.[5] Country butchers, i.e. those who were not citizens, held markets in the mid-sixteenth century within Leadenhall on Wednesdays and Saturdays when they rented stalls at 8*d*. a week. The citizen butchers later forced the closure of the Wednesday market so that at the time when Alley was writing the country butchers were constrained to sell their beef, lamb and mutton only on Saturdays.[6]

It is not clear whether the street market for non-citizen producers of victuals was held daily or only on Saturdays. Alley suggests that the vendors came, not only from London, but from Middlesex, Surrey, Kent and Essex also. Alley depicts a range of foodstuffs on sale: grain, cuts of meat, pigs' heads, sausages, poultry and, perhaps, fruit and vegetables. But it is clear that meat and poultry were the main produce. In 1595 the City discussed the possibility of making room within Leadenhall for mealmen to sell their meal under cover, and near to the office of the meal-weigher. But it proved impossible to persuade the wool merchants to make room so Alley depicts a man standing with his sack of grain out in the street.[7]

NOTES

[1] Harben, p. 345; E. Ekwall, *Street-Names of the City of London* (1954), p. 95; Stow, i, p. 160. See above, p. 10.
[2] Stow, i, p. 160.
[3] A. H. Thomas, 'Notes on the History of Leadenhall 1195–1488', *LTR*, 13 (1923), pp. 1–22.
[4] Stow, i, pp. 159–60; Harben, p. 344.
[5] CLRO, Rep. 23, ff. 471v, 474v, 551v. In 1587 Leadenhall had been in a ruinous condition, CLRO, Rep. 21, f. 420v.
[6] P. E. Jones, *Butchers*, pp. 89–90, see above p. 11. *Analytical Index to the series of records known as the Remembrancia . . . 1579–1664* (1878), p. 202.
[7] CLRO, Rep. 23, ff. 471v, 474v, 551v; Rep. 24, f. 128v; the Court of Aldermen waged a campaign against the Merchants of the Staple and attempted to take possession of the lofts and rooms which they occupied at Leadenhall in 1598–99, see CLRO, Rep. 24, ff. 319v, 328, 418v–9, 420v, 463r–v; Rep. 25, ff. 7v, 9v, 21v.

f. 13v BRODE STRETE p. 62

The Alderman on the right is Sir Stephen Slanye, a skinner, who had served as mayor in 1595–6 and so is shown wearing a chain of office. At the time of Alley's drawing he was serving his fourth term as master of his company. Later he was to act as president of Bethlem, Bridewell and Christ's hospitals and then, from 1604–8, as surveyor-general of all the City hospitals. He died in 1608.[1]

The deputy, on the left, was probably Nicholas Barnesley, a grocer, who had been elected the previous year. He served on his company's court of assistants in 1599 and was warden the following year. In the city he was a governor of Bridewell, and of St Bartholomew's hospitals. He seems to have lived in the parish of St Christopher le Stocks where he acted as auditor in 1577, churchwarden in 1581, and assessor for various parish subsidies in 1586–91. He was also involved in collecting the subsidy in Broad Street ward.[2]

NOTES

[1] Beaven, ii, p. 42.
[2] Benbow, Index; Edwin Freshfield, *The Vestry Minute Books of the Parish of St Bartholomew Exchange* (1890), p. 39.

f. 14 STOCKS p. 63

The Stocks market is seen here from the west. The façade with the two doorways faced onto Poultry. But, uncharacteristically, Alley has also depicted the northern façade of the building which faced onto Cornhill. The two roads shown on the left of the picture are probably Cornhill with Broad Street leading off from it.

On the right of the drawing Alley shows the church of St Mary Woolchurch which lay to the south of the Stocks market building. In 1442 the church had been extensively rebuilt and a new north wall constructed fifteen feet away from the Stocks market. Between the church and the market house there was a footway leading from the east end of the Stock market through to Poultry and above the footway there was the parsonage house.[1] Alley's drawing bears out the information to be found in the fifteenth century deeds very exactly. From left to right, therefore, Alley has shown the north façade of the Stocks market, the west façade, the parsonage house built over a common footway and then the church of St Mary Woolchurch itself. Alley has drawn the church with a tower which is also depicted on the copperplate and 'Agas' maps.[2]

Although the Stocks market was first built in the thirteenth century the building shown here was constructed *c*.1406–11.[3] In 1543 there were 25 'boordes or stalls' for fishmongers and 18 for butchers, which together brought in a rent of £82 3*s*.; this was spent on the maintenance of London Bridge.[4] By 1596 the market was leased out as a whole to a farmer, who then sublet the stalls, but he was not allowed to let any single stall for more than £3 6*s*. 8*d*. The farmer paid the City £56 4*s*. in rent.[5] In 1645 the market was described as a 'great stonehouse' which had rooms, or stalls, for the sale of flesh to the north of the west door, and for the sale of fish to the south.[6] This division would seem to be that shown by Alley. Whereas the butchers displayed their wares on rails beneath an overhanging pentice, the fishmongers used trestle tables, or 'boordes'. This same distinction can be observed between the fishmongers of New Fish Street and the butchers of Eastcheap (see ff. 11, 19). In the fifteenth century the rooms above the shops had been let out to chaplains, but later they were simply let to those who wanted them.

NOTES

[1] *CLBK*, p. 272; see also Derek Keene, ed., *Historical Gazetteer of London before the Great Fire*, 2 (Walbrook) forthcoming. This will include an account of the properties in the parish of St Mary Woolchurch, and the account of the church will be found under the reference 118/0.
[2] *A–Z*, 23, CP 2.
[3] Keene, op. cit.: the account of the Stocks market will be found under reference 118/17.
[4] Stow, i, p. 226.
[5] CCPR, Stocks; When John Catcher leased the Stocks market in July 1601 he was to bear the cost of repairs but was allowed to charge the stall-holders 1½*d*. per foot of shop. Needless to say there were complaints about Catcher, and his son Edward, CLRO, Rep. 25, ff. 263v–5, 273v, 278, 301, 323; Rep. 26, ff. 65v–66v.
[6] Sydney Perks, *The History of the Mansion House* (1922), pp. 63–4.

f. 14v   CHEAPE WARDE   p. 64

The Alderman on the right is Stephen Soame, a girdler, who had not yet served as mayor, although he was to succeed Saltonstall in October 1598. After being elected mayor, Soame chose to transfer from the lesser company of Girdlers to the great company of the Grocers. The Girdlers were so incensed at this move that they removed Soame's arms from their hall. He came from a minor Norfolk family but had made a very considerable fortune in London as an Eastland merchant and founder member of the East India Company. He invested widely in land, largely in south-east England, and provided each of his four sons (he also had five daughters) with a landed estate. Soame chose to be buried at Little Thurlow in Suffolk where he built and endowed almshouses and a free school. In London he served as an MP in 1601 and was involved with the administration of the City's hospitals. When he died in 1619 he left money to a number of London charities and he had also paid for the glazing of the great north window in St Paul's Cathedral.[1]

John Pinder, the deputy for Cheap ward from 1594–1602 was a man of some considerable importance in the City. Together with Soame he was elected MP in 1601 and, in the following year, paid a fine to avoid service as sheriff, thereby ensuring also that he would not be called upon to serve as alderman or mayor. He did, however, act as an auditor from 1595–1601 and as a governor of Bridewell Hospital. While he was a common councilman he served as a member of the City Lands Committee and on thirty-five other committees. In 1594 he was given the task of overseeing the building of the City's new pest house (or plague isolation hospital) in Moorfields.[2] He served both as warden and as master of his company, the Vintners. Pinder rented the Mitre tavern in Cheapside from the Mercers' company, and lived in the parish of St Mary Cole-church, in the ward, where he died in 1608. In his will he left money to several city charities and requested burial in the Mercers' chapel.[3]

NOTES

[1] *H of C*, iii, pp. 414–15; Beaven, ii, p. 43.
[2] CLRO, Rep. 23, ff. 262, 331.
[3] *H of C*, iii, p. 266

f. 15   CHEAPESIDE MARKET   Plate II and p. 65

The market here is seen from the south. On the left, or west, of Alley's drawing is shown the church of St Michael le Querne; the elaborate pillar structure further east is Cheap Cross; further east again is the Standard and on the right hand side of the drawing is the Great Conduit which stood in front of Mercers' Hall. At least seven lanes led northwards from this part of Cheapside but Alley has chosen not to depict any of them but to show instead a schematic row of two storey houses, although we know from the almost contemporary drawing by Ralph Treswell that the houses were, in fact, of two, three or four storeys on the north side of Cheapside.[1]

The church of St Michael le Querne (i.e. atte Corn, or where corn is sold)[2] was enlarged in 1429–30 and the City then undertook responsibility for maintaining the conduit which stood at the east end of the church, although it is not depicted by Alley. Ralph Treswell drew the church and the conduit in 1585 with rather more care and accuracy than Alley, but both artists show what appears to be a clock at the east end of the church looking towards Cheapside.[3]

The Cheap Cross, or Great Cross, was really a decorated pillar surmounted by a cross erected in about 1296 by Edward I in memory of his queen, Eleanor. It was rebuilt, or renovated, several times in the fifteenth century, and was regilded in 1522, 1533 and 1554, but then it was defaced in 1581. A year after Alley's drawing, in 1599, it was taken down, but then restored again in the following year and finally demolished in 1643.[4] The restored Cross is shown on an engraving of the entry of Marie de Medici to London in 1638.[5]

The Standard contained a water conduit within it and was in existence by the late fourteenth century. It had been a favourite spot for executions; for example Wat Tyler beheaded the rich vintner, Richard Lyons, here during the Revolt of 1381, but in the sixteenth century it was the scene of public, but less drastic, punishments. The early Standard was of wood, but it was rebuilt in stone c.1430–3.[6] Although Alley depicts the Standard as being as large as, if not larger than, the Cheapside Cross, other representations (e.g. the 'Agas' woodcut map and the 1638 engraving) show the Standard as considerably smaller than the Cross.[7] Stow described how the Standard was decorated with 'wells imbraced by angels', the badge of John

Wells (d. 1442), by whose benefaction it was largely rebuilt in the fifteenth century.[8]

The Great Conduit shown on the right of Alley's drawing was built in the middle of the thirteenth century and was probably the City's first public water conduit. It was repaired in 1378 by the executors of the mercer, Adam Fraunceys, and was in further need of repair a century later.[9] Alley appears to show a single storey building with projecting pipes, or spouts, a pitched roof over the cistern and some sort of tower. The copperplate map of the 1550s seems to show a two tier water supply from a square, castellated cistern.[10] Stow described the Great Conduit as 'castellated with stone, and cesterned in leade'.[11]

The water for the Conduit outside the church of St Michael le Querne, for the Standard, and for the Great Conduit, was brought in lead pipes from Paddington. In Ralph Treswell's drawing of the church of St Michael he clearly depicts three pipes coming from the west; one of them turns into the little conduit outside St Michael's church and the other two continue eastwards, presumably to serve the Standard and the Great Conduit and other conduits further east. The centrality of Cheapside and later, perhaps, the availability of water, explain its popularity as a market. In 1588 the vegetable-sellers in Cheapside were forbidden to wash their goods in the street 'for we find by experience that that leads to great anoyance and hath byn some cause of infection'.[12]

Cheapside was a wide street lined by shops held by citizens, but the street market in the middle of the thoroughfare was predominantly used by country vendors to sell their produce. Alley suggests, by the names on his pillars, that the vendors will come from Middlesex, Essex, Kent, Surrey and Hertfordshire. Although in 1588 the City restricted the sellers of flowers, herbs, roots, and seeds to the western end of the market between St Michael le Querne and the Cross, and the foreign sellers of victuals to the stretch between the Cross and the Great Conduit, it would not seem that this division has been observed in Alley's drawing and may well not have been observed in practice.[13] Subject to certain restraints, hucksters and hawkers, who were street-walking sellers, particularly of food, were allowed to buy food in the markets for resale.[14] Alley may have depicted a huckster with her pannier and a hawker with his basket on his back, leaving the market with their purchases.

Commentary

NOTES

[1] See John Schofield, *The London Surveys of Ralph Treswell* (LTS, 1987), plate 1.

[2] Harben, pp. 411–12.

[3] Schofield, *Treswell*; cf. Howard Colvin, 'Inigo Jones and the church of St Michael le Querne', *London Journal*, 12 (1986), pp. 36–9.

[4] Howard Colvin (ed.), *History of the King's Works*, I (1963), pp. 479, 483–4; Harben, p. 471; P. Norman, 'Abstracts of Documents...', *LTR*, 6 (1909), pp. 76–9.

[5] Reproduced in Derek Keene, *Cheapside before the Great Fire* (ESRC pamphlet, 1985), pp. 8–9.

[6] Harben, p. 545.

[7] Keene, *Cheapside*, pp. 8–9, 21; see also the copy of the view of Cheapside in 1547, ibid., pp. 10–11.

[8] Stow, i, p. 26.

[9] Harben, p. 271.

[10] *A–Z, CP* 2.

[11] Stow, i, p. 264.

[12] CLRO, Rep. 21, f. 543.

[13] Ibid.

[14] Above, p. 6.

f. 15v   FARRINGTON WITHIN   p. 66

The alderman shown on the right is, presumably, Richard Martin, a goldsmith who became alderman of the ward of Farringdon Within in 1578, but then moved to Bread Street ward in 1598. His successor at Farringdon Within was Humphrey Weld, who was sworn on 9 May 1598. Weld had not yet served as Mayor and so the alderman depicted by Alley wearing a chain of office must be Martin, who had already served twice as mayor. This helps us to date Alley's work since it was compiled after Saltonstall was knighted (March 1598) and before Martin moved to Bread Street in May of the same year.

Richard Martin was born in 1534 and when he was only twenty-five he became a Warden of the Mint and then, in 1581, Master. He retained this office until his death in 1617 at the age of eighty-three. While master he was active in devising schemes to improve royal finances by increasing the revenue from the Mint. Martin appears to have pursued a wide range of economic opportunities: he was named in the charters granted to the Levant Company, owned salt works and was a dominant figure in the Society of Mineral and Battery Works.[1] He was

knighted in 1589 and was involved in the management of the City's hospitals. In 1594 he became a goldsmith to the Queen. But although he retained the Mastership of the Mint until the end of his life, in 1602 he became so poor that he was imprisoned for debt and was removed from all his civic offices including his aldermanry. He lived, and died, at Tottenham and was a governor of the local free school at Highgate.[2]

The deputy shown here is probably Thomas Bankes, a barber-surgeon, who was elected in 1583 and served until his death in 1598. Bankes had been a Common Councilman of the ward since 1582 and served on a record-breaking seventy-one committees, including the important City Lands Committee in 1592–3. He acted also as a City auditor in 1589 and as a Commissioner for Bankruptcy in 1595–6. He was a warden and then master of his company. Bankes lived in the parish of St Michael le Querne, within the ward, where he was elected constable in 1575 but, like many of his contemporaries, he paid a fine not to serve. He was, however, prepared to act in the more prestigious offices of churchwarden, vestryman and auditor. When he died in 1598 he left the lease of two shops to the parish.[3]

NOTES

[1] Lang, 'Aldermen in Business', pp. 243, n. 6, 257.

[2] Beaven, i, p. 40; *DNB*.

[3] Benbow, Index.

f. 16   ST NICHOLAS SHAMBELLS   p. 67

The Shambles, in the parish of St Nicholas Shambles (replaced in 1547 by the enlarged parish of Christchurch Newgate Street), consisted of two rows of butchers' shops lying back to back in the middle of Newgate Street, and known as Middle Row.[1] The southern row of shops, or stalls, was known as the back side, and the northern row simply as the Shambles. Alley appears to be depicting one of the rows of butcher's shops, together with some of the houses in Newgate Street, probably from the south. Unlike the butchers of Eastcheap those in the Shambles did not have slaughter houses attached to their shops or stalls, and so they killed beasts in the street to the north and south of Middle Row. This led to problems for traffic, as well as sanitation, and 1516 the slaughtering of beasts in the Shambles was prohibited by royal injunction.[2]

Citizen butchers in London had been selling their meat in the Shambles since the twelfth century.[3] Originally they had movable stalls, but by the early sixteenth century, Middle Row already consisted of fixed tenements or shops, as Alley shows. Stow described how the butchers originally sold their 'flesh meat' from 'stall boordes' over which 'they first builded sheades to keepe off the weather, but since that incroching by little and little, they have made their stall boordes and sheads, faire houses, meete for the principall shambles'.[4] The meat sold here, as in Eastcheap, was predominantly beef, mutton, veal and pork, and the carcasses of cattle and pigs can be identified hanging up outside the shops on rails. It would seem that whole carcasses and large cuts of meat were sold here, whereas the smaller joints, or cuts, of white meat were sold in the City's more general markets like Cheapside.[5]

NOTES

[1] Harben, pp. 412–13.
[2] P. E. Jones, *Butchers*, pp. 76–82.
[3] Ibid., pp. 74–5; see above, p. 1.
[4] Stow, i, p. 343.
[5] Ibid., i, p. 313. The Shambles are shown on the plan of the Greyfriars precinct drawn in 1617 and reproduced by J. E. Price, 'On recent discoveries in Newgate Street', *TLMAS*, 5 (1885), p. 420.

f. 16v Untitled p. 68

Alley has not given a name to the ward in which Newgate market was situated, perhaps because it straddled two wards, Farringdon Within and Castle Baynard. Since Alley has already depicted the alderman and deputy of Farringdon Within, it may be reasonable to assume that we have here the alderman and deputy of Castle Baynard. The alderman at this time was Edward Holmedon, a grocer, who had been master of his company in 1596–7, when he was also elected alderman. In the year following Alley's drawing, he was elected sheriff, but he never served as mayor, although he was knighted in 1603. He served on the committee of the East India Company and

then, in the year in which he received his knighthood, he ceased to be an alderman. He did not, however, die until 1616.[1]

The deputy of Castle Baynard ward at this time was John Parr, who had been elected in 1587 and held the office for fifteen years. He was also acting as a governor of Bridewell Hospital at this time. Parr lived in the parish of St Benet Paul's Wharf, close to the Royal Wardrobe situated in the adjoining parish of St Andrew, which was convenient since he held the office of King's Embroiderer. Parr served as a vestryman and church-warden of his parish and died in 1605.[2]

NOTES

[1] Beaven, ii, p. 46.
[2] Benbow, Index.

f. 17 NEWEGATE MARKET p. 69

The market is seen here from the north: on the right Alley has shown Newgate (a schematic drawing, compare with f. 23) and, on the left, the western end of Middle Row (see f. 16). Alley has drawn with some care the market house which was built by the City in 1547 when Sir John Gresham was mayor.[1] Six years later the country victuallers were ordered to use the 'new buildings lately made'.[2] In 1588 the pavement lying between the market house and Newgate itself was levelled and repaired.[3] Clearly the market was much used and the new market house had to be enlarged in 1591 to accommodate more meal and corn. While the building work was in progress the meal-sellers were allowed to use the parish church of Christ-church nearby, except during divine service![4] Stow described the newly enlarged market house as 'A faire new and strong frame of timber covered with lead' and an open, arcaded building, corresponding quite closely to that drawn by Alley, is shown on the map of the Greyfriars precinct drawn in 1617.[5]

Before the building of the market house most of the buying and selling took place on the pavement inside Newgate. By the fourteenth century it was both a grain market and a general market for country producers and in the sixteenth century both these activities continued.[6] Alley's drawing would suggest that grain and meal was stored and sold in the new market house, while the general market of country produce continued to take place on the pavement between the market house and Newgate. The names on Alley's pillars would suggest that the country vendors, selling 'butter, cheese, fruit, ... veal, pork, bacon, sowse, and other victuals'[7] came from Middlesex, Kent and Surrey as well as from London itself.

NOTES

[1] Stow, i, p. 343.
[2] CCPR Newgate Market.
[3] CLRO, Rep. 21, f. 542v.
[4] CLRO, Rep. 23 (i), ff. 50, 54v; Rep. 22, ff. 280v, 315v, 329.
[5] Stow, i, p. 343; J. E. Price, 'Recent discoveries', *TLAMAS*, 5 (1885), p. 420. See also the 'Agas' map, *A–Z*, p. 8.
[6] See above, p. 10.
[7] CLRO, Letterbook Q, f. 186. The reference is to an order of 1543 concerning Newgate, Cheapside, and Gracechurch markets.

f. 17v FARRINGTON WITHOUT p. 70

The Alderman on the right is Paul Bayning (or Banning), a grocer. He had served as sheriff in 1593–4 and in 1599 moved from Farringdon Without (a notoriously difficult, and poor, ward) to Walbrook where he served until 1602. He was active in the East India Company and died in 1616.[1]

Since Farringdon Without was such a large and unruly ward it seems to have needed three deputies. We do not know the names of all the three deputies who were acting in 1598, nor do we know which one Alley depicts here. It could be Florence Caldwell who was active as deputy of the ward in 1599 and may well have been serving earlier. He acted as common councilman from 1586 until 1603 and served on twenty-one committees, including the City Lands Committee from 1600–6. Caldwell was a City Auditor in 1599 and was active in the government of Bridewell Hospital. He belonged to the Haberdashers' Company and served on the Court of Assistants in 1592 and as warden the following year. Six years later he paid a fine in order not to have to serve a second term as warden. Caldwell was also active within the parish of St Martin Ludgate where he lived 'without the gate'. The boundary between the wards of Farringdon Within and Farringdon Without lay along the city wall, but the parish of St Martin, the church just within the city wall at Ludgate, extended outside

the wall and so Caldwell could be a parishioner of St Martin and also live in the ward of Farringdon Without, where he served as deputy.[2]

Another man who may have been serving as a deputy in the ward at this time was Mathew Martin. He had been elected as a deputy in 1596 but there is little evidence of his acting in this capacity subsequently and he may have died soon afterwards. He had been a common councilman since 1587 and had also served as a governor of St Bartholomew's Hospital. Martin was by trade a brewer and he acted both as a warden and then as master of his company. He lived within the ward in the large parish of St Sepulchre.[3]

NOTES

[1] Beaven, ii, p. 44.
[2] Benbow, Index.
[3] Ibid.

f. 18 SMITHFELD p. 71

Alley has drawn the topography of Smithfield with considerable care and accuracy, if without much sense of scale or perspective. The open space is seen from the east so that the fencing, or bars, shown lying across the road on the right are Smithfield bars which lay at the northern end of the field, blocking the road which led to Charterhouse and Clerkenwell. If we move from right to left across the top of the drawing, i.e. down the west side of the field, we come first to the pens for animals. The road to the north (i.e. right) of the pens is Chick Lane and the road to the south Cow Lane. Both these lanes led westwards towards Holborn. Following around the field we come next to Hosier lane (just above the horseman's head) which also led west to Holborn, and then to Rennerstreet which ran south to Newgate. The block of houses on the left of Alley's drawing, i.e. the south, is interrupted by the great gate which led into St Bartholomew's Hospital. At the bottom left-hand corner of his drawing (i.e. the south-east) Alley shows Duck Lane which ran between the Hospital and the Priory of St Bartholomew. The west gate, or main gate, into the Priory is shown in the next schematic row of houses. The Priory was dissolved in 1539 but much of the church still survives. The final lane which Alley shows leading out of the field at the north-east is Long Lane, which led eastwards towards Aldersgate Street and Finsbury Fields.

Since the twelfth century Smithfield had been the City's main market for the sale of live animals, whether horses for riding, or beef, sheep and pigs for eating. By the sixteenth century it was the only place within the City's jurisdiction where non-citizens were allowed to buy, or sell, livestock.[1] Although the open space at Smithfield was probably being encroached upon by housing and the trees had disappeared, it was still an important open market.[2] The sheep pens had become a permanent fixture in the market by the middle of the sixteenth century and in 1568 the City leased them out for twenty-one years at a rent of £20 p.a. The lessee then leased out the pens on market days (Wednesdays and Fridays) for 6*d.* each.[3] Just to the east of the pens lay the Horsepool which Alley does not show. Doubtless it was used for watering the animals but was filled up after the Great Fire.[4]

The bars which lay across the street to the north of the open space existed as early as the twelfth century, and possibly earlier. They marked the boundary between the liberty of the City and the county of Middlesex.[5] Alley has carefully depicted two butcher's shops which lay just north of the bars and outside the City's jurisdiction. Smithfield was not one of the recognized markets for butchers, but this restriction would not apply beyond the limits of the City's jurisdiction. Indeed the City may have owned these butchers' shops for in 1586 the Corporation leased a butcher's shop adjacent to Smithfield bars.[6]

Although Alley appears to have placed the gateway to the Hospital on the south side of Smithfield, and that to the Priory on the east side, with reasonable accuracy, yet both the drawings seem to be wholly schematic. The gateway to the medieval hospital was pulled down in the early eighteenth century and rebuilt in the classical form which it has today.[7] The Priory gatehouse was, presumably, destroyed in the course of the secularization of the Priory buildings. The gateway that exists now is, in fact, the remains of the south-western doorway of the Priory church surmounted by a sixteenth-century timber building.[8]

Whereas the other horses depicted by Alley seem to be solid beasts of burden moving at a respectable pace through the City's streets (e.g. ff. 9, 10, 12, 15) this horse in Smithfield is being ridden by a young blood going at a gallop, recalling the equestrian sports which Fitzstephen described at Smithfield in the twelfth century.[9]

NOTES

[1] See above, p. 11.
[2] Stow, ii, p. 29.
[3] CCPR, Smithfield.
[4] Harben, p. 308.
[5] Ibid., pp. 325, 536.
[6] CLRO, Rep. 21, ff. 304, 383.
[7] Royal Commission on Historical Monuments, *London*, vol. iv (1929), p. 160 and Plate 206.
[8] Ibid., p. 165 and Plate 206.
[9] Printed in Stow, ii, p. 223; 'Agas' shows similar activity, *A–Z*, p. 8.

---

f. 18v   Untitled   p. 72

Here again Alley seems to have been uncertain in which ward the fish market in Old Fish Street lay because the street formed the boundary between the two wards of Queenhithe and Bread Street. Since Alley later draws the alderman and deputy of Queenhithe ward, these two men may be presumed to belong to Bread Street. The Alderman on the right was Benedict Barnham, the son of Francis Barnham, another Alderman and draper. By 1572 Benedict had spent some time at St Alban Hall at Oxford and two years later he purchased the freedom of the City in the Drapers' Company which he served as master in 1592–3. He had become both a sheriff and the alderman of Bread Street ward in 1591 and he was frequently consulted by the Privy Council about London matters. Although he was never an MP for the City he sat for Minehead in 1588–9 and for Yarmouth in the Isle of Wight in 1598–8. Barnham died on 4 April 1598, just as Alley was compiling his book. His will contains many London bequests and reveals that he had extensive landed property in Essex, Hampshire, Kent and Middlesex, as well as in London. He did not live in Bread Street ward, but in the parish of St Clement Eastcheap where the church was dominated by the monuments of Benedict and his father.[1]

John Ireland was chosen as deputy for Bread Street ward in 1598 and served for three years. He had been a common councilman since 1585 and had served on a number of committees. In 1601 he became a governor of St Bartholomew's Hospital and he may have died not long after this. He was a salter, but there is no record of his having held office in his company, nor in his parish of St Mildred Bread Street.[2]

NOTES
[1] *H of C*, i, p. 398; Beaven, ii, p. 44; Stow, i, p. 218.
[2] Benbow, Index.

f. 19   OULDE FISHESTRETE   p. 73

It is not clear whether Alley is showing this market from the north or the south. Old Fish Street formed the central section of the very long street known as Knightrider Street which extended from Atheling Street lying south-west of St Paul's to Le Riall, or Royal Street on the east side of the Vintry. The section of the street called Old Fish Street ran from Old Change to Candlewick Street, with several lanes leading off to north and south, which Alley has omitted (as he did in his Cheapside drawing, f. 15). It seems likely that Alley has here depicted the row of fishmongers' shops which stood in the middle of Old Fish Street, as the butchers' shops (Shambles) stood in the centre of Newgate street (f. 16). This row of shops in the middle of the street did not extend the whole length of Old Fish Street but only from Old Change as far as Bread Street.[1]

The fish market in Old Fish Street had been one of the three places designated by the City for the retail sale of fish (the others being New Fish Street (Bridge Street) and the Stocks (see ff. 10, 14), but it was open only to citizens.[2] It served as the fish market for the western parts of the city and its supplies arrived at the Old Fish Wharf and Queenhithe. Stow wrote 'In this old Fishstreete, is one row of small houses, placed along in the middest of Knightriders streete ... these houses now possessed by Fishmongers, were at the first but moveable boordes (or stalles) set out on market daies, to shew their fish there to be sold: but procuring license to set up sheds, they grew to shops, and by little and little, to tall houses, of three or foure

stories in height, and now are called Fishstreete'.[3] The shops shown by Alley seem, however, to be only of two storeys and not three or four.

NOTES
[1] Harben, p. 449.
[2] See above, p. 8.
[3] Stow, i, p. 346.

f. 19v   QUEENHITHE WARDE   Plate III and p. 74

The alderman shown on the right is John More (or Moore), a skinner who had only been elected as alderman in January 1597. At the time of Alley's picture More was serving as sheriff and so is shown wearing the sheriff's chain of office, which appears to be a diminutive form of the chain of office worn by an ex-mayor. More was master of the Skinners' Company in 1597 and 1601 and also served on the committee of the East India Company. He died in April 1603.[1]

The deputy for Queenhithe ward here shown by Alley may have been Paul Hawkins, who was a common councilman of the ward from 1597 and is to be found acting as deputy by 1599. He served as a governor of Christ's Hospital from 1597 and on the committee for the poor of the ward in the following year. He was a vintner and served as warden in 1596 but later transferred to the Mercers' Company. He was a parishioner of Holy Trinity the Less, Queenhithe, and served his parish church both as a vestryman and as churchwarden in 1596. He died in 1600.[2]

NOTES
[1] Beaven, ii, p. 46.
[2] Benbow, Index.

f. 20   QUEENEHITHE MARKET   Plate IV and p. 75

The market and dock of Queenhithe are seen here from the north, that is from Thames Street. The dock area is shown as being wider, but less deep, than the Billingsgate dock (see f. 9) and the boats which are using the landing place seem to be river boats rather than the sea-going vessels which Alley has shown sweeping into Billingsgate. Alley also depicts some steps leading down to the water on the east side of the dock.

Although in the fifteenth century the landing place at Billingsgate which lay below London Bridge seems to have become more important than Queenhithe, yet there are signs that Queenhithe was again becoming busy in the sixteenth century. The grocer Sir John Lyon (d. 1564) left a bequest of £100 towards the cost of building a market house at Queenhithe and this is the arcaded building which Alley shows.[1] At the same time the wharf was walled in stone (shown perhaps on the extreme right of the picture) and the work completed by 1566.[2] In 1591 the market house was enlarged by the addition of a penthouse which is probably the range of attic housing shown above the arcade.[3] Stow described the building as 'one large house for stowage of corne craned out of Lighters and Barges'[4] but Alley does not, unfortunately, depict any of the cranes. The shields which have been carefully shown above the pillars of the arcade probably displayed the arms of Sir John Lyon. Alley has also indicated that the market area was enclosed with houses to the north and east and a fence on the west. Gateways into the market are shown on the north and west.

The only commodity which Alley has displayed in the market is sacks of grain and the sale of this was, indeed, the original purpose of the market, although salt was also sold there by the fourteenth century.[5] Although fish was landed there, it was taken to Old Fish Street (f. 19) for sale. But after the completion of the new market house in 1566 the City decided that Queenhithe should serve not only as a market for meal, wheat and grain brought by water to the City from the west, but also for the sale of onions, garlic, salt, apples and other fruit.[6]

The new market house was let to the meal weigher at a rent of 40 marks p.a. in 1578, but in 1591 the office of yeoman of the meal market and keeper of the market house was farmed at £40 p.a.[7]

NOTES

[1] Stow, ii, p. 10; CLRO Rep. 15, ff. 399, 513v; 16, ff. 117v.
[2] CLRO, Rep. 14, ff. 331, 409v.
[3] CLRO, Rep. 19, ff. 331, 498; f. 472v; 22, ff. 198v, 245, 248v, 257, 269.
[4] Stow, ii, p. 10.
[5] See above, p. 9.
[6] CLRO, Rep. 16, ff. 133r–v.
[7] CCPR, Queenhithe.

f. 20v BRIDGE WITHOUT p. 76

The ward of Bridge Without had been created as recently as 1550 when the government of the borough of Southwark was entrusted by Edward VI to the Lord Mayor and Corporation of London. In fact, by this royal charter, only three of the five manors of which Southwark was composed fell under the control of the City. The disorder which continued to reign in the other two manors and the anomalous survival of a manorial structure within the three manors which made up the new ward, meant that the alderman and his deputies had a particularly difficult task.

The alderman at this time was Richard Goddard, a draper, who had been elected in 1595. Four years later he moved on to Dowgate and then moved again in 1602 to Walbrook where he died two years later. He served on the committee of the East India Company and was knighted in July 1603 when James I – presumably in a naïve excess of enthusiasm – honoured seventeen of the Court of aldermen in this way.[1]

The Ward of Bridge Without had three deputies, one of whom at this time may have been Richard Hutton, an armourer, who was serving in the early 1590s. But as he was dismissed from office as bailiff of Southwark in 1595, he is likely to have been dismissed from his other offices at the same time.[2]

NOTES

[1] Beaven, i, 256; ii, p. 46.
[2] Stow, ii, p. 69; CLRO, Rep. 24, ff. 429r–v.

f. 21 SOUTHWARE MARKET p. 77

The section of Borough High Street shown here by Alley was, in the sixteenth century known as Long Southwark. The view is taken from the east, so London Bridge lies to the right of the picture.

The market in Southwark had originally been associated with the hospital of St Thomas and was held, from the thirteenth century onwards in the street outside the Hospital which lay on the east side of Long Southwark.[1] This market declined in the fifteenth century, probably from competition from a weekly market established in the high street by the City, which had acquired extensive rights within the central portion

Commentary

of Southwark which the City had acquired from the Crown by a series of royal charters in 1406, 1442 and 1462.[2] This area over which the City had jurisdiction was known as the Guildable Manor. The City's market extended on the west side of the street as far south as St Margaret's church, but on the east side of the street only as far as the Swan Inn which marked the boundary of the precinct of St Thomas's Hospital and also the limits of the Guildable Manor.[3] By the middle of the sixteenth century the market was becoming overcrowded and impeded traffic. The Leet Court in 1548 attempted to impose some order by regulating the 'standings' of vendors: they allocated places to fishwives (who sold from baskets), fish stall-holders, butchers, country poulterers, grain sellers, herb wives, fruit-erers, and bakers and poulterers from London. Hucksters who bought up market goods for resale could only do so after 11 a.m.[4]

The new charter which the City obtained from the Crown in 1550 not only extended the jurisdiction of the City from the Guildable manor to two of the remaining four Southwark manors, but also gave the City the right to hold a market in Southwark on four days a week (Monday, Wednesday, Friday and Saturday) and to take fees from stallholders.[5] The two bailiffs of Southwark, appointed by the City, were responsible for supervising the market. In 1552 the bailiffs were to account to the City for the profits, but in 1557 they were entitled to keep them.[6] In 1552 four men were appointed to assist him in the sale of fish and meat there.[7] The market was used not only by the inhabitants of Southwark itself, but by London victuallers and also country producers. The names on Alley's pillars suggest that these country vendors may have come from Middlesex, Essex, Kent and Surrey.

The pillory which Alley has drawn so prominently was certainly in position by the 1530s, and probably earlier. From references to it in the Southwark Court Book (1539–64) it seems to have been particularly used for market offenders.[8] In 1606 a new pillory and stocks were provided at the cost of the Bridgewardens.[9] From Alley's drawing it would appear that the offender was shut into an elevated cage, rather than standing on the ground, or it may be that Alley simply forgot to draw the lower halves of his offenders!

The bell seems always to have been a feature of the Southwark market. The bailiff rang the bell at 2 p.m. in winter and 3 p.m. in summer, to close the market.[10] When a new bell was needed in 1554 it was, again, the Bridgewardens who bore the cost.[11] In the earlier sixteenth century there was no market house for the Southwark market but, as at Newgate and at Queenhithe (see ff.17 and 20) a market hall was built in the course of the century. The exact date for the construction of the Southwark market house is not known but it appears to have been built in the last quarter of the sixteenth century, probably on the site of the market bell. A new bell was built onto the roof of the market house as Alley shows. Before the building of the market house, farmers who brought grain from the countryside to sell were obliged to have their sacks weighed first at the King's Beam (which may have been kept at the bailiff's house) and then to display them for sale near the pillory. After the building of the market house, the Beam was kept there and the vendors were provided with some protection for their produce. The market house had to be enlarged in 1606, for which the Bridgewardens paid, and it was then destroyed by fire in 1676.[12].

NOTES

[1] Martha Carlin, 'The Urban Development of Southwark, *c*.1200–1550', unpublished PhD thesis, University of Toronto, 1983, pp. 156–7.
[2] Ibid., pp. 466–74.
[3] Ibid., p. 158.
[4] Ibid., p. 159.
[5] Ibid., pp. 473–4.
[6] David J. Johnson, *Southwark and the City* (1969), p. 185.
[7] Ibid., p. 305.
[8] Ibid., p. 297. The Southwark Court Book is in CLRO, MS. 39C.
[9] Johnson, *Southwark*, p. 128.
[10] Ibid., p. 310.
[11] Ibid., p. 128.
[12] Ibid., p. 305 and notes 4 and 5.

f. 21v   BISSHOPES GATE   p. 78

This view of Bishopsgate is taken it would seem from outside the City. This, and the three following drawings, seem not to have been executed with the same attention to detail as the more general views of the City markets. There is little evidence that any of the gates drawn by Alley looked very much like his pictures.

Bishopsgate was one of the city's six main gates: it lay on the north-eastern section of the city wall, giving on to the old North Road leading into Hertfordshire and Cambridgeshire. It had been rebuilt by the Hanse merchants in 1479. The merchants had been willing to repair the gate again in 1551 but since their privileges in England were withdrawn in 1552 the 'worke was stayed' and the old gate was still in use when Stow wrote.[1] The copperplate map of 1559 shows the south, or inner face, of the gate with a single niche for a statue.[2] There appear to have been two gateways, a central one with an arch and portcullis, with a smaller pedestrian arch lying to the west. Strype, in his edition of Stow's *Survey* published in 1720, described the gate, with its 'old statues'. Above the gateway, both the north and to the south, were statues of bishops; in addition on the north, or outward face, there were two statues of kings.[3] Strype also provides an engraving of the gate but it bears very little resemblance to Alley's drawing.[4] The gate was rebuilt in 1721 and then finally destroyed in 1760.[5]

NOTES

[1] Stow, i, p. 32.
[2] *A–Z*, CPI.
[3] John Strype (ed.), *A Survey of the City of London by John Stow* (1720), i (pt. 1), p. 17.
[4] Ibid., plate facing p. 14.
[5] Harben, p. 75.

f. 22 LUDGATE p. 79

This view is probably taken from outside, i.e. to the west, of the gate. See the comments on f. 21v.

Ludgate was one of the six main gates of the city, on the west side giving access to the Strand and Westminster. In the late fourteenth century the gate had been made into a gaol for London citizens so that they should not have to suffer the horrors of Newgate prison. In 1463 Agnes Foster, the widow of the mayor Stephen Foster, enlarged and improved the prison and provided an endowment so that the prisoners should not, in future, have to pay for their lodging or for water.[1] In 1586, ten years before Alley's drawing, the gate had been 'cleane taken downe' and the whole gate 'newly and beautifully builded', with a statue of King Lud on the east side and of Queen Elizabeth on the west, at a cost to the citizens of some

£1,500.[2] Nothing of this splendour permeates Alley's drawing and it bears little resemblance to the engraving of the gate made by Strype in 1720.[3] Whereas Alley's gate looks, if anything, medieval, the gate drawn by Strype was firmly classical. Both drawings, it should be pointed out, show the gate surmounted by a cupola. Along with the other City gates, Ludgate was finally demolished in 1760.[4]

NOTES

[1] Stow, i, pp. 39–40.
[2] Ibid., pp. 38–9. See also Betty R. Masters (ed.), *Chamber Accounts of the Sixteenth Century* (LRS 20, 1984), pp. 181, 201; payments totalling £1,651 11s. 11d. were made in 1585–6 to William Kerwyn freemason for the rebuilding of the gate and part of the gaol of Ludgate. The rebuilding seems also to have included the provision of a 'double dial' clock.
[3] Strype, *Survey*, i, (pt. 1), plate facing p. 14. Strype also adds that the statues were still in place when he wrote and that King Lud was accompanied on the east side of the gate by his two sons, although the inside of the gate which had been of timber had been burnt in the fire of 1666. Since then it had been repaired and provided with a chapel for divine service: ibid., p. 21.
[4] Harben, p. 372. All four of the Ludgate statues are now at the church of St Dunstan in the West.

f. 22v ALGATE p. 80

Alley's drawing of Aldgate seems to be even more sketchy than his drawings of the other city gates. It must have been the oldest of the city gates by the end of the sixteenth century since there is no record of its having been rebuilt between 1215 and 1607–9. In 1374 the rooms above the gate had been leased by the City to Geoffrey Chaucer and a hundred years later the defences of the gate were strong enough to withstand an attack led by Fauconberg in 1471 in the Lancastrian cause.[1] It seems clear, however, that by the time that Stow was writing the gate had become decrepit: of the two pairs of gates, only one now remained and, in the same way, only one of the portcullises was still in place; 'the other wanteth but the place of letting downe is manifest'.[2] The gate is shown on the 'Agas' map of c.1562 where it is depicted as a low square structure, flanked by two semi-circular towers. The presence of such towers is corroborated by Symonds's plan of Holy Trinity Priory, drawn c.1592, which shows the semi-circular northern tower.[3] Strype describes the magnificent new gate of the early seventeenth century, adorned

Commentary

on its eastward, or outer face, with two fearsome soldiers and a statue of King James, and on its western or inward face, figures of Fortune, Peace and Charity.[4] The gate was taken down in 1761, along with the other city gates, and although it was re-erected at Bethnal Green, nothing now remains either of the structure or of the statues.[5] Aldgate opened into Whitechapel and the eastern suburbs, and gave access to the main road through Essex into Suffolk, both counties important suppliers of London's foodstuffs.

NOTES

[1] *CLBG*, pp. 327–8; Stow, i, p. 30.
[2] Stow, i, p. 29.
[3] *A–Z*, p. 12; Symonds's plan is reproduced in Harben, plate 4.
[4] Strype, *Survey*, i (pt. 1), p. 16 and see plate facing p. 14.
[5] Harben, p. 9.

---

f. 23   NEWEGATE   p. 81

Alley appears here to have taken a little more trouble to depict Newgate. Both the gate and the adjoining gaol were rebuilt in 1423–32 by the executors of Richard Whittington.[1] It would seem that this early fifteenth century gate was the one still in use in the late sixteenth century. Unusually Stow says nothing at all about the condition, or appearance, of the gate in his day.[2]

Newgate does, however, appear on the 1617 map of the Greyfriars precinct and the drawing there is not dissimilar to Alley's picture here.[3] It would seem that Newgate had two square towers at either side of a lower central section and that the building was crenellated. In 1630–1 the eastern, or inward, side of the gate was rebuilt, but then the whole gate was destroyed in the fire of 1666.[4] It was again rebuilt but, judging by the engraving of the rebuilt gate to be found in Strype, it would seem that some of the medieval features remained within the new structure:[5] Alley's drawing, the Greyfriars plan, and Strype's engraving all have features in common. The gate was finally removed in 1777 and the prison was rebuilt at this time. The gaol was finally pulled down in 1902.[6] The road from Newgate, after descending to cross the Fleet, ran westwards to become, eventually, the Oxford Road.

NOTES

[1] Jean Imray, *The Charity of Richard Whittington* (1968), pp. 8–9.
[2] Stow, i, pp. 35–7 describes past events connected with Newgate, but not its present condition.
[3] J. E. Price in 'Recent Discoveries', *TLMAS* 5 (1885), p. 420.
[4] Strype, *Survey*, i (pt 1), p. 19.
[5] Ibid., plate facing p. 14; but compare Alley's drawing of Newgate here with the rather different representation of the gate to be found on f. 17.
[6] Harben, pp. 432–3.

INDEX

South Ockendon, Essex, 82
Southwark, 20, 25, 96–7; bailiff of, 96–7; Guild-able Manor, 97; Leet Court, 97
Southwark market, 5, 9, 11, 33, 96–7, **77**; bell, 97, **77**; market house, 33, 97; pillory, 33, 97, **77**; stocks, 97
'sowse', 10, 93
Spencer, Sir John, clothworker, Lord Mayor, 25
spices, 9, 24
Standard in Cheapside, 10, 33, 90
Star Chamber, court of, 18–21
Statutes, 18–22
  relating to informers, 18–19; market offences, 18, 23; price of beer, 18
Stocks market, 4–8, 10–11, 32–3, 88–9, 95, **63**; farmer of, 89 and n. 5; reconstruction drawing of, 33
stocks, in Southwark, 97
stones, 84
Stow, John, author of *A Survey of London* (1598), 16, 31, 33, 84–8, 90, 92, 95–6, 98–9
Strand, 98
straw, 4
Strype, John, editor of John Stow's *Survey of London* (1720), 98 and n. 3, 99
Sturdevant, Matthew, swordbearer, 82
subsidy assessments, 20, 28
Suffolk, 18, 21, 99
Surrey, 87–8, 90, 93, 97
surveyors of beer, 16, 24
Sussex, 18, 21, 87
Swan Inn, Southwark, 97
swordbearer, 34, **51**; dress and duties of, 82
Symonds, John, his plan of Holy Trinity Priory, 98, 99 n. 3

T

Tallow, 23–4, 26
  assizes of, 23, 26
Tallow Chandlers' Company, 19

Thames Street, 85, 95
Thomas, Robert, draper, Deputy of Candlewick Street ward, 86, **56**
Threadneedle Street, 4
Thwayte, William, fishmonger, Alderman of Bishopsgate ward, 86, **58**
Tottenham, 91
Tower Street, 86
  ward, 85
Treharne, Philip, 28
Treswell, Ralph, surveyor, 31, 34, n. 1, 90
Tyler, Wat, 90

V

vegetable markets, 9–10, 90
  sellers, 90
vegetables, 10, 12, 88
  garlic, 96
  herbs, 9–10, 12, 90
  onions, 84, 96
  roots, 9–10, 12, 90
  seeds, 12, 90
Vintners' Company, 89
Vintry, 95

W

Walbrook, 1, 4
  ward, 93, 96
Waleys, Henry le, Mayor, 4
wanderers, 31
Wardmote Inquests, 19, 22, 24, 26
Warren, Sir Ralph, 83
waterbailiff, 22, 28
waterfowl, 10 and n. 87
water supply for City, 90
weighing,
  beams, 24, 25, 27, 84, 88, 97

meal weigher, 88, 96
weights and measures, 17, 22, 24–5
wool weighing, 5
Weld, Humphrey, Alderman of Farringdon Within ward, 34, 91
Wells, John, 90
Westminster, 17, 20, 34
  local government in, 17–18
  markets in, 5
Westminster Abbey, 17, 28
Whitechapel, 99
Whitehall palace, 17
Whittington, Richard, mercer, Mayor, 84, 99
Wilbraham family, 29–31
  Major Hugh Edward, 29
  Richard, Common Serjeant (d. 1601), 29–30; Elizabeth [Pullyson], wife of, 29
Wilkinson, Rowland, minstrel, 24, 28
wine, 4, 7, 22, 26
  assizes of, 22, 26
wood, 18, 26
  assizes of, 22, 26
wool, 88
  merchants, 88 + n. 7
Woolchurchhaw, 4
woollen cloth, 9
worsted cloth, 5, 87
Wyatt, Joanne, 17
Wyngaerde, Anthony van, 31, 84

Y

Yarmouth, Isle of Wight, 94
Yarmouth (Norfolk) fishermen, 8
yarn, 11
Yeomen of the Chamber, 22
  of the Channel, 22–3
  of the Waterside, 22, 24–5
  of the Woodwharves, 22, 28
Yorkshire, 87